MW01156781

REAL
POWER

REAL POWER

∾

RISE ABOVE YOUR NATURE
AND
STOP FEELING ANGRY, ANXIOUS, OR INSECURE

DOVID LIEBERMAN, Ph.D.

REAL POWER. Copyright © 2008 by D. Lieberman. All rights reserved.
No part of this book may be used or reproduced in any form or by any
means, or stored in a database or retrieval system without prior written
permission of the publisher except in the case of brief quotations embod-
ied in critical articles and reviews.

Published by: Viter Press, 1072 Madison Avenue, Lakewood, NJ 08701

Email DavidJay@aol.com   Fax: 772-619-7828

ISBN Hardcover: 978-0-9786313-3-8

ISBN Softcover: 978-0-9786313-5-2

Library of Congress Control Number: 2007922712

PRINTED IN THE UNITED STATES OF AMERICA

שמואל קמנצקי
Rabbi S. Kamenetsky

2018 Upland Way
Philadelphia, Pa 19131

Home: 215-473-2798
Study: 215-473-1212

January 10, 2007

I was presented with part of this book's pre-publication manuscript. I believe that much benefit could be derived from reading this material and I encouraged the author to continue in this very important endeavor.

Every human being is created with the ability to choose good or evil. The Torah states, "See — I have placed before you today the life and the good, and the death and the evil" and "...you shall choose life..."

Dr. David Lieberman shows us the intricate and magnificent connection between the choices we make and the quality of our lives. He illuminates the wisdom of the Torah in a practical, easy to understand and enjoyable presentation

This book will leave you with a greater understanding of yourself and others, and a stronger desire to follow in the ways of the Almighty.

Shmuel Kamenetsky

CONTENTS

FOREWORD

*"God made man straight, but they sought
many calculations."*

—ECCLESIASTES 7:29

The pursuit of emotional wellbeing is a universal goal. Unfortunately, few people seem to attain it. In some situations, the quest carries us further from, rather than closer to, emotional health.

Some people try to achieve fulfillment in life by way of empty pursuits. Others seek to escape from life through overindulgence in physical pleasures or by endless distractions and forms of entertainment. Not only do these pursuits ultimately diminish real happiness, they eventually result in even greater distress. Not finding what you are looking for on this course should inspire you to change your direction.

Once, Rabbi Levi Yitzchok of Berdichev stopped a person who was scurrying about the marketplace. The Rabbi asked him, "Where are you going?" "I can't talk with you now," the man exclaimed, "I am running after my *parnossa* (livelihood)." Rabbi Levi Yitzchok inquired further, "How do you know that you are running *towards* your *parnossa*? Maybe your *parnossa* is in the other direction," the rabbi proposed, "and you are running away from it."

Many people pursue objectives along paths that lead nowhere. Instead of avoiding these futile paths, they follow them again and again. One definition of insanity is doing the same thing and expecting different results.

A man was once lost in the forest. He met another man and asked that man if he would show him the way out of the forest. But the second man replied, "I, too, am lost. Although I cannot show you the way out, I can show you which ways *not* to go, because I've tried them, and they lead nowhere." That is insanity.

In *Real Power,* Dr. Lieberman draws on Torah wisdom as well as psychological principles to demonstrate which paths in life should be followed, and those which should be avoided. He examines and clarifies the themes of self-confidence, perspective, and free will. If you truly desire to turn self-doubt into self-esteem (and who doesn't?), I urge you to read *Real Power* carefully. It will set you in the right direction. This is a terrific book.

—Rabbi Abraham J. Twerski, M.D.
Founder and Medical Director Emeritus,
Gateway Rehabilitation Center

INTRODUCTION

*"I have put before you, life and death . . .
choose life so that you may live."*
—DEUTERONOMY 30:19

Technological advancements have made our lives increasingly comfortable, safe, and easy; and we have more opportunities and advantages available to us today than ever before.

Given the high level of both opportunity and comfort, one would expect people to be happier than ever, and even more satisfied with their lives. The reality, though, is startlingly different. Instead of thriving and feeling empowered as a result of greater choices, we are deteriorating.

According to the latest research, one in four Americans suffers from mental illness.[1] The drug companies

---

1. The National Mental Health Information Center.

try to keep pace, with the sales of anti-depressant, anti-anxiety, and mood-stabilizing drugs at record levels, and tens of millions of new prescriptions being written each year.

But that doesn't seem to be enough.

Many people are finding life just too painful. Every day, 80 Americans take their own lives, and over 1,900 Americans visit Emergency Departments for self-inflicted injury.[2] Sadly, more teenagers and young adults die from suicide than from cancer, heart disease, AIDS, birth defects, stroke, pneumonia and influenza, and chronic lung disease, combined.[3]

So why are we suffering from such emotional pain and anguish? Drawing on the wisdom of Torah and fundamental principles in psychology, *Real Power* offers insights into the human condition, and reveals how regardless of the opportunities available to us today, a lack of self-control results in poor choices, and ultimately leads to negative emotions and destructive habits.

As a solution, *Real Power* offers neither exercises or affirmations, nor meditations or motivating mantras. There is no homework to do or journals to fill out.

2. National Hospital Ambulatory Medical Care Survey, total 706,000.
3. According to studies, industrialized countries tend to have a higher suicide rate than poorer, developing countries.

Rather, readers learn how to **regain self-control** and move their thoughts, choices, and lives in a purposeful, powerful, direction, free from the shackles of anxiety and stress.

SECTION

I

THE TRUTH
ABOUT REALITY

CHAPTER 1

A GLIMPSE OF REALITY

> *"One must guard his mind more than any-*
> *thing else, for it produces all the results*
> *of life."*
>
> —MISHLEI 4:23

What makes some people capable of handling life's challenges with quiet calm and optimistic resolve, while others
dissolve at the slightest insult or frustration? The answer
has to do with our perspective: how we see, feel, behave,
and, ultimately, respond to circumstances in our life.

Imagine a small child playing with a toy that suddenly breaks. The child's whole world is shattered, and
she may respond by crying, or by becoming frustrated,
sad, or even angry. The child fails to appreciate, let alone
recognize, that she is still being clothed, fed, loved, and
taken care of—not to mention that there is a whole
world outside of her own smaller world. The child's

parents know that the broken toy has no significance, but the parents have perspective that the child lacks.

Intellectually, we may know that what makes us anxious or upset is actually unimportant and insignificant. The qualities however, that most of us strive to exemplify— such as objectivity, calm, and patience—are lost to annoyance and impatience when, in a hurry, we encounter the checkout clerk with the trainee name-tag staring at the cash register as if it were the cockpit of a 757. We try to maintain our cool, but negative emotions surface, and once sparked, blaze. Now we face an uphill battle.

Techniques such as taking deep breaths, reciting affirmations, or practicing visualization, might work when we face minor issues, but they're insufficient for life's really big challenges.[4] Reminding ourselves not to get annoyed is not a solution. Yes, the objective is to remain calm, but this is better accomplished through not becoming agitated in the first place. When we fight the urge to blow up or melt down, we battle our own nature.[5]

4. Affirmations can be a powerful tool in reshaping our self-image. However, an effective short-term therapy called Neo-Cognitive Psychology, advises that reciting positive affirmations can be counterproductive while we are in a negative state. This is because we are charging the thought with negative energy. Instead, we should verbalize an affirmation only when we are in either a neutral or positive state.

5. When we desire to change our behavior, particularly when it goes against our natural inclinations, it is as effective as being told that we need to alter our past behavior. No one would suggest trying to rewrite

Without perspective, we are forever like the child hold-ing the broken toy.[6] This is why we often become irritated in the heat of an argument. After a few moments, our anger subsides. A few hours later, we are less angry, and in a few days, we wonder why we were so bothered in the first place. Time provides perspective, allowing us to see the situation with clarity.[7]

Likewise, as we grow older and look back on certain events and incidents in our lives, we realize that the car we (as young adults) felt we *must* have, the person we *must* go out with, or the job we *must* land, simply aren't "musts" anymore.

history, yet we believe that we have more control over how we will behave and respond to similar circumstances in the future. This is the inherent shortcoming of motivation. We can feel excited, and desire to make a change, but the enthusiasm soon wears off when we find our-selves frequently unable to continue to behave in a way that is inconsis-tent with who we are. Like a spring, we will stretch only so far before snapping back to our original positions

6. Perspective is one of the three translations of the *sefirah* of knowledge (*da'at*). In this particular context, *da'at* is the key that opens and closes the chambers of the heart, the seat of emotion. In the language of the Sages, "Without *da'at*, there is no separation (*havdalah*)" (*Berachot* 33a). In today's language and this context, this means that, without perspec-tive, a person cannot disengage (i.e., separate) from his own emotions and stop himself from being "suffocated" by them.

7. "Accept a teacher upon yourself" (Ethics of the Fathers 1:16). No matter how a great a person is, there is no escaping some bias. Making wise choices can often be less about knowledge, and more about having the ability to see the situation clearly.

When we discover how to shift perspective, we see the events of today through the lens of tomorrow. Once we can recognize what really matters, we will no longer need to force ourselves to remain calm. Our thoughts, feelings, and responses to any critical situation reshape themselves. Negative emotions like impatience, insecurity, anger, and worry dissolve—not because we fight to control our emotions, but rather because we realize that the circumstances are inconsequential.

THE LENS OF PHYSICS

6

The ability to shape our emotional state is not simply a matter of looking through rose-colored glasses. Rather, reality itself changes when we shift perspective.

Quantum mechanics provides insight into two fascinating discoveries about the nature of energy and our universe. Quarks—subatomic particles that make up atoms and are the building blocks of creation—have two unique properties. One is that particles are changed when they are observed. As unusual as this seems, it is impossible to observe the particle's true nature, because the very act of observation actually changes what it is. Second, quarks can appear in two places at once. They are not confined to one location at one time. Our discussion will focus primarily on the former quality.

Perspective does not make us see reality differently; on a quantum level, it creates our reality. Where you are "standing," your vantage point, determines what is brought into existence.[8] Since the observation of an event changes it, we recognize that our perspective changes our objective reality, because our perspective alters our place of observation.[9] Physicists agree, then, that we do not interface with our environment as separate entities. More accurately, we affect reality as if we were a single organism.

8. Researchers at Israel's Weizmann Institute of Science revealed that the greater the amount of watching of these subatomic particles, the greater the observer's influence on what actually takes place. (A 1998 study reported in the February 26 issue of *Nature*, Vol. 391, pp. 871–874.) In effect, this is why we cannot, in an instant, recreate our reality. The watching that we speak of is qualitative in nature, not quantitative. The significance of this is that the ability to be in the moment, whole, and focused is more necessary a condition to affecting reality, than the mere amount of time spent vaguely daydreaming a particular existence.

9. The power of the mind is astonishing. A myriad of studies show that a person with multiple personality disorder—an illness in which two or more distinct personalities inhabit a single body—can manifest traits, desires, memories, abilities, eye color, and even separate IQs for each personality. Documented cases show that each personality also manifests its own brainwave and voice patterns. Each personality can have individual medical disorders, such as asthma, or even diabetes, while the other personality shows no signs or symptoms.

CHAPTER 2

SHIFTING PERSPECTIVES

"All is foreseen, but freedom of choice is given."

—ETHICS OF THE FATHERS 3:19

Within human beings, three inner forces exist and are often at odds with each other: the body, the ego, and the soul. In short, the body wants to do what *feels* good; the ego wants to do what *looks* good;[10] and the soul wants to do what *is* good.[11] When the alarm clock goes off in the

10. The ego is also called the yetzer hora, or evil inclination, and is identified with nefesh, the soul's lowest level. When the ego is engaged, it deceives us in four primary ways: (1) It chooses that on which we focus; (2) it makes what we see all about us; (3) it concludes that all negative experiences are due to a deficiency within ourselves—albeit often unconsciously; (4) it causes us to believe that we can think our way out of a situation that is beyond our control.

11. The soul's influence is called the yetzer tov, our good inclination, or conscience. Kabbalah classifies four levels of the soul: *nefesh, ruach, neshama,* and *neshama l'neshama. Nefesh* is the animating principle of

morning, the three forces all battle it out.[12] If we hit the snooze button, guess who won the first round? Doing what is easy or comfortable is a body drive. Examples of overindulgences of this force are overeating or oversleeping—in effect, doing or not doing something we know we should or should not do, merely because of how it feels. Basically, the body just wants to escape from it all.[13]

---

the physical body and the senses; *ruach* is the force vitalizing the emotions; *neshama* is the vitality of intellect; and *neshama l'neshama* (or chaya) is the essence of life of the human soul. However, these levels of the soul are often regarded as extensions of the essence of the soul (which may be considered a fifth level) called *yechida*.

12. From the ensuing internal conflict, these forces combine to create free will. Specifically, free will is the moral component of each decision—the right and wrong. For example, whether or not you wiggle your right finger or left finger right now is not so much of a function of free will. Yes, it is a choice, but one that has no moral consequence. Free will is most easily found in the gap between what we know we should do and what we feel like doing. If we know that we should help a friend, but instead feel like watching TV, we experience a free will battle between the soul and the body. If we want to make a comment to impress one person at the expense of embarrassing another, we experience a battle between the ego and the soul. However, to walk over to an older lady and clunk her over the head with a brick is not a free will choice, because this is outside the scope of our reality. It is not really a choice we should need to make. We hope.

13. We know that eating the entire container of ice cream will make us feel nauseous in about five minutes, yet we continue to dig in, knowing that we will soon regret our actions. Such is the lure of transitory delights.

An ego drive can run the gamut from making a joke at someone else's expense to buying a flashy car that is beyond our means. When we are motivated by ego, we do things that we believe project the right image of ourselves. These choices are not based on what *is* good, but on what makes us *look* good.

If we cannot control ourselves and we succumb to immediate gratification or strive to keep up an image, then we become angry with ourselves, and feel empty inside. To compensate for these feelings of guilt and inadequacy, the ego engages and we become egocentric. As a result, our perspective narrows, and we see more of the self and less of the world; this makes us increasingly more sensitive and unstable.

We only gain self-esteem when we are able to make responsible choices, and do what is right, regardless of what we feel like doing or how it appears to others—this is a soul choice.[14] In turn, we rise to a higher and healthier perspective, because self-esteem and the ego are inversely related; like a see-saw, when one goes up the other goes down.

While our mood will inevitably fluctuate as a result of our circumstances, our emotional wellbeing remains

---

14. This doesn't mean we should ignore our body's basic needs. Nourishing the body and enjoying physical pleasure is absolutely in keeping with Judaism. Abuse or overindulgence, however, is not healthy, and leads to the deterioration of our wellbeing.

largely immune from conditions and experiences of all types, positive and negative.

Research indicates that big lottery winners often lead miserable lives after their windfall.[15] A statistically uneven number of suicides, murders, drunk-driving arrests, divorces, even bankruptcies that befall "winners" have led to studies of a lottery curse.[16] People find it

---

15. Brickman, P., Coates, D.F., Janoff-Bulman, R. (1978). "Lottery winners and accident victims: Is happiness relative?" *Journal of Social and Personality Psychology* 36, pp. 917–927. In this same study, researchers revealed that although people have strong emotional reactions to major changes in their lives, these reactions appear to subside more or less completely, and often quite quickly. After a period of adjustment, lottery winners are not much happier (and some are even quite miserable) when compared with a control group. Equally compelling is that recent paraplegics were themselves not much unhappier than the control group.

The Torah offers an insight into this psychological phenomenon. "Again she [Leah] conceived and bore a son and declared, 'This time I will thankfully praise Hashem'" (Genesis 29:35). The Talmud says: "From the time of creation there was no person who praised God until Leah came and thanked him upon the birth of Yehudah" (*Berachot* 7b). Certainly there were others who expressed appreciation to God, but none contained this unique quality. Rav Avraham Pam explains that when one achieves a happy milestone in life, such as marriage, a newborn child or a financial achievement, one's heart overflows with joy and gratitude. Yet, as time passes one gets used to the good fortune and the joy begins to dissipate. Knowing this as well, Leah named this fourth son Judah, a derivation of the Hebrew word hoda'ah, meaning "praise." This way she would always remember to thank God for her blessings.

16. "Since you are eating and satiating yourself, be careful lest you turn away from God, for one tends to turn away from God when he is sated"

difficult to comprehend why such misfortune follows those who suddenly become so fortunate.[17] The reason is quite clear. Since self-esteem comes from making good choices, we (with instant money or fame) now have more ammunition for greater unconstructive behavior and indulgences.[18]

Logic therefore dictates that if we are in control of ourselves, and act responsibly, we can never be deeply bothered by anyone or anything. We are not a casualty of anything other than our own behavior, because nothing affects us; we affect everything.[19]

(Rashi, Deuteronomy 11:16, from *Sifri* 43). See also Deuteronomy 8:12–14. Moses foretold the future and warned the Jews that they would "become fat . . . and . . . desert God . . ." (Deuteronomy 32:15).

17. "Most instances of good and misfortune in this world are dependent upon character traits" (Vilna Gaon, *Even Shleimah* 1:7).

18. The Rambam (*Shemoneh Perakim* 3) explains that just as there are cholei haguf (people who suffer from physical affliction), there are also cholei hanefesh (people who suffer from emotional or spiritual sickness). Just as one who is physically sick will eat things that are potentially harmful to him, a person who is a *choleh nefesh* will engage in behaviors that are potentially harmful using his negative *middot* (character traits) and other ills to satiate himself.

19. The Rabbis say that, to a large extent, before a person is born God decrees whether that person will be clever or foolish, strong or weak, healthy or diseased, rich or poor. Only whether the person will be a *tzaddik* (a righteous person) or a *rasha* (an evil person) is not preordained; that depends on free will (*Niddah* 16b). We may choose whether to be good or bad, and we only need that choice in order to gain all that we could ever want.

Choosing Our Reality

Each circumstance is like a blank canvas until we paint the picture with our thoughts, which then give rise to our emotions.[20] For instance, when a person acts rudely towards us, it doesn't *mean* anything. It only tells us that the person does not like who he is; not that there is something wrong with us. This person's words or deeds "cause" us to feel bad about ourselves because of *our* self-image.

If a crazed person starts screaming at us, it is unlikely that we will be negatively affected by the encounter, but what about a close friend or colleague?[21] We fear that the person in question no longer likes or respects us.

14

---

20. Even beyond our emotions, we often mistakenly substitute our thoughts for reality. Dr. John Sarno, professor of clinical rehabilitation medicine at New York University School of Medicine, states in his book, that, "I have never seen a patient with pain in the neck, shoulders, back or buttocks who didn't believe that the pain was due to an injury, a 'hurt' brought on by some physical activity . . . The idea that pain means injury or damage is deeply ingrained in people's consciousness. Of course, the pain starts while we are engaged in physical activity but, as he explains, "that is often deceiving" (Sarno, John E. *Healing Back Pain.* Warner Books. 1991).

21. This is why we are often more hurt when we feel disrespected by someone who is smart, wealthy, or attractive. We unconsciously believe that this person has more value and is better, so his words and deeds carry a greater impact. "Everything is according to the shamer and the one being put to shame" (*Bava Kamma* 83B).

Even if our fears are founded, what does his or her opinion really have to do with our self-worth? Nothing.

We often, unconsciously, look to the situation to determine how personally we should take what is happening. For example, a car cuts us off on the road, and we are curious to see what the driver looks like. Why? Because we want to see if this is someone who looks like he would do such a thing to us on purpose. A little old lady sitting in the driver's seat would not enrage us as much as a young male smoking a cigarette with music blaring from his car's open windows. This is because most of us would assume that the old lady simply didn't see our car while the young male *did it to us* on purpose.[22]

It is good to keep in mind that the more arrogant a person appears to be on the outside, the more vulnerable and helpless he is on the inside; and while we have a harder time connecting with the reckless driver because of his demeanor, we must recognize that our ego is the indicator of how well we see the reality beyond the façade.[23]

---

22. Compassion naturally emerges for children, the elderly, the sick, or even animals, because we more easily see their vulnerability—via their appearance.

23. When a person exhibits a tremendous degree of self-sacrifice and puts his own needs or even his life to the side for another, we get that lump-in-the-throat feeling. Why? Because that person has set aside his own ego; he has given of himself to do what is right for another person, and so we are touched. This is a connection, though, that is not borne

ANOTHER ANGLE

Linguists recognize a sentence that is illogical if it is semantically incorrect. Consider the statement, "My friend forced me to have blue eyes." No one would accept this sentence as truthful. However, we easily accept the declaration, "My friend makes me angry." Both statements, though, are semantically identical, and according to linguists, structurally incorrect.

A short-term therapy called, Neuro Linguistic Programming (NLP) recognizes the need to identify such destructive patterns, because of their inherent tendency to pervade our subconscious thoughts. The creators of NLP offer the following overview as an aid, designed for therapists, to recognize when this behavior is present:

> We have generalized the notion of semantic ill-formedness to include sentences such as:
> *My husband makes me mad.*
> The therapist can identify this sentence as having the form:
> *Some person causes some person to have some emotion.*

out of a sense of the other's vulnerability, but rather his soul's infinite goodness. The wall of "I am me and he is he," is broken down; and where there is no ego, there is connection.

When the first person, the one doing the causing, is different from the person experiencing the anger, the sentence is said to be semantically ill-formed and unacceptable. The semantic ill-formedness of sentences of this type arises because, it, literally, **is not possible for one human being to create an emotion in another human being**—thus, we reject sentences of this form. Sentences of this type, in fact, identify situations in which one person does some act and a second person *responds* by feeling a certain way. The point here is that, although the two events occur one after another, there is no necessary connection between the act of one person and the response of the other. Therefore, sentences of this type identify a model in which the client assigns responsibility for his emotion; rather, the emotion is a response generated from the model in which the client takes no responsibility for experiences which he *could* control.[24]

We assume that an event is to blame for our feelings; this is not so. The senses take in stimuli which are then given meaning by one's thinking. Unaware of the

---

24. Bandler, Richard and Grinder, John: *The Structure of Magic.* Science and Behaviour Books Inc. (1975).

process, a person mistakenly equates these perceptions with reality.[25]

We must be abundantly clear on this point: the meaning we assign to a situation is based on how we feel about ourselves—and unless we feel differently about ourselves, which can only come through a change in behavior,[26] we cannot see the world differently. Our perspective is locked into place, unless we unlock it by making more effective choices.

18

25. "Reality can best be described with a metaphor of the mind as a film projector. Our thoughts then become the film through which the light-carrying sensory stimuli shines. Consciousness is the light which causes the images on the screen to appear as real." (Mills, R.C. *Realizing mental health: toward a new psychology of resiliency.* Sulzberger & Graham. 1995).

26. It is more accurate, though possibly misleading, to use the word "intentions" instead of "behavior." We know that one who honestly intends to perform a mitzvah, though thwarted, still gets credit for it (*Berachot* 6a). However, we often speak of having good intentions without truly expecting to act on them.

CHAPTER 3

TIPPING THE BALANCE
OF FREE WILL

> *"Be as fierce as a leopard, light as an eagle,*
> *swift as a deer, and strong as a lion to ful-*
> *fill the will of your Father in heaven."*
> —ETHICS OF THE FATHERS 5:23

While intellectually we understand the power of choice, as human beings we are at the whim of our egos, and despite Herculean efforts to respond objectively and calmly to a situation, we nonetheless fail far too often.

As long as our self-image is unchanged, then the response will be consistent every time, fluctuating within a narrow band based on our mood. This is especially true in "constricted consciousness" (a kabbalistic term for a bad mood), where it is nearly impossible for us to pull ourselves out of our ego-oriented state, see clearly, and then behave appropriately.[27]

---

27 We cannot *directly* eliminate or even diminish our ego, since the unconscious screams out in protest if we do anything that deviates from

God Lights up Reality

God gives us *flashes of perspective* that temporarily enhances our ability to see clearly and so it becomes easier, in that moment, to make a better choice. For example, after witnessing a serious accident, what happens? We do not feel like joking. We are quiet. We feel almost detached, separated from the illusion of the world. So much seems irrelevant . . . at least for the moment.

how we see ourselves. To be humble by putting ourselves in humbling situations is like a person choosing to sleep the night in a homeless shelter: while positive, it is voluntary. He is in control and, as such, is not really humbled. In fact, he may now think to himself, look what I was able to do. Beating down the ego will not eliminate it; it only causes the ego to re-engage and to fight, and our efforts will be largely ineffective. A person, having been thrust into a situation where he is not in control and where he maintains self-control by exercising free will, gains lasting humility. To manufacture conditions where we are dependent does not really improve our character—since it was our free will to enter that situation.

God has created our world in such a way that there are plenty of opportunities to exercise self-control and to diminish our egos every day. A wealthy person begging for money on the street has only a mild opportunity to enhance his humility.

On the other hand, when the same person is in a naturally humbling situation—for example, he finds himself on the street without his wallet, and instead of becoming frustrated and upset by his inability to give charity, he rises above his nature—he gains a real opportunity for growth. (This final point is sourced in *Orchot Tzadikim 2* [*Sha'ar Anavah*].)

We gain perspective and are simultaneously filled with gratitude and humility. Thus, we gain self-control in that instant. We do not care who is there, who looks, or who stares. We do not judge or want or crave. The ego loses its pull, and its voice is muted.

The psychological mechanics—the actual process—behind perspective is intriguing. Let us see how this works:

A person sustains severe injuries in an accident and then works tirelessly to regain the use of his legs. He will likely have immense and lasting gratitude for his subsequent ability to walk. On the other hand, the gratitude of someone who narrowly averts an accident dissipates after just moments. Shouldn't the more fortunate one be more grateful than the injured person? After all, he didn't need to endure painful surgeries and struggle through months of rehabilitation. Even more amazing, the person who had never needed to swerve to avoid an accident (and possibly incur a lapful of scalding coffee) typically feels little, if any, gratitude.

It's odd, isn't it, that the one who survives and triumphs over disaster is filled with lasting gratitude; the one who sidesteps the accident feels fleeting gratitude and perhaps even annoyance; and when nothing happens at all, we simply complain about the traffic. What's going on here?

The reason that gratitude is so often fleeting is that we believe what we have is deserved—we have a sense of *entitlement.* If we found ourselves in a war zone and managed to reach our destination safely, we would likely be grateful. But, if we do not perceive traveling as a physical threat, then getting from point A to point B unharmed has little significance. Indeed, why should we feel grateful for something we have come to expect? This is how it *should be.*[28]

It's only when reality *conflicts* with expectations that we realize our "inalienable rights" can suddenly be denied. The person who drives uneventfully experiences no threat to his wellbeing. From his perspective, life is as it should be. But, after a near miss, he recognizes that *the possibility of unfulfilled expectations exists*, so he feels some gratitude that his perceived entitlements were not taken from him. This effect is even greater after an accident because his world, his reality, has changed forever.[29] His

28. King David ended the Book of Psalms with the verse: "All souls will praise You," which the Sages interpret as, "For every breath that a person takes, he should praise God," for nothing can be taken for granted. The prayer of gratitude, *Nishmat Kol Chai*, was based on this last verse. It is a *segula* (a seemingly symbolic action that has the potential to produce a positive ramification well beyond the natural consequence of the action itself) for good health, livelihood, marriage, children, and success in all endeavors.

29. This is why someone can put off going to the doctor for years, even when a troublesome symptom is hard to ignore. As soon as the appointment is made, anxiety and worry grow exponentially; the symptoms become more pronounced because the person has incorporated the real possibility of "finding something" into his reality. This is the reason a

ability to walk is not guaranteed, so when he regains the use of his legs, he sees it as a *gift*.

The greater our perspective in life, the more permanent and deep is our gratitude. Nothing needs to happen to make us feel good. We simply appreciate what we have. To the degree we are egocentric we are constantly angry and frustrated at life for coming up short. Our expectations are never met, and we are consumed with what we lack, and what is owed to us. Happiness eludes us, and we are always one step away from feeling complete as we search endlessly for the next thing that promises to bring us lasting fulfillment.[30]

23

Capturing Inspiration

After the terrorists attacks of September 11, 2001, many people began to question the direction and purpose of their lives. In fact, a record number of people sought therapy; an increase of drug and alcohol abuse was also reported. Beholding the delicate, finite, and temporary nature of the world makes us want to attach ourselves to something more, something real.

---

person delays making a desired purchase for many months and then, when he finally orders it, willingly pays more for expedited delivery. 30. A person who feels emptiness on the inside seeks to be filled by things on the outside and will always need more. "No man leaves the world with half his desires fulfilled" (Ecclesiastes 5:9).

If we are doing something that is truly fulfilling, then our resolve is enhanced. However, if our pursuits are myopically selfish or simply unfulfilling and uninspiring or, in the context of reality, simply insignificant, then we are driven, at least temporarily, to do something that gives more meaning to our lives. Often, we resolve silently to do something, but that sentiment fades in time, and we go back to our old ways and old thoughts.

Most people allow the momentum to dissipate.[31] When the clarity fades, so does our steam; the opportunity is lost unless we take possession of it.[32] The objective is not simply to gain an incremental movement forward—only movement in the physical world opens the next window. Consider multi-leg airline travel to a remote location. If we miss one of our flights, then we lose the opportunity for the connecting flight. Whether or not we take action, our reality unfolds in accordance with our expectations. When we tell ourselves that our desire (enthusiasm or will power) won't last anyway, then we let the moment pass and we prove ourselves right. The truth, however, is that we missed our next spiritual flight by not moving in the physical world.[33]

24

31. The Mesillat Yesharim explains that a person's enthusiasm and inspiration to act does not translate into action because of lack of zerizut (energetic action).
32. "If not now, when?" (Ethics of the Fathers 1:14).
33. "King David said, in Psalms 119:60, "I was quick; I did not delay in

There is no such thing as procrastination in the universe. Each action produces a reaction, uninterrupted, unless it is acted on by another force, which itself produces a reaction. Motion creates emotion; since we live in a physical world, the physical needs to be engaged while inspiration touches our soul.[34]

As Rabbi Moshe Chaim Luzzatto writes in The Path of the Just (*Mesillat Yesharim*):

> Furthermore, zeal can result from an inner burning in the same way that it creates one. That is, one who perceives a quickening of his outer movements in the performance of a *mitzvah*, conditions himself to experience a flaming inner movement, through which longing and desire will continually grow. If however, he is sluggish in the movement of his limbs, the movement of his spirit will die down and be extinguished . . . For as a result of willed quickening of his move-

25

keeping your *mitzvot*." King Solomon (Proverbs 22:29) said, "Have you seen a man quick in his work? He will stand before kings. He will not stand before low-life." In Genesis 18:11, the Zohar comments that each day in a person's life carries its own challenge and mission. What is to be accomplished today cannot be postponed until tomorrow because tomorrow has its own set of things to do.
34. *Mesillat Yesharim* 1.

ments, there will arise in him an inner joy and a desire and a longing.

It is not enough to nurture strong *feelings*; we can only effect change by *doing*. The purpose of creation is to unify the spiritual and the physical, elevating the latter, not to discard one form or the other.

Taking immediate swift action actually *transforms* that action, allowing us to accomplish much more. This is not just because we have more time, but because the action is qualitatively different as a result of our moving sooner and more quickly.[35] When we get up early, for example, we gain more than just an extra one or two hours; rather, the experience of the entire day is simply different, more elevated.

While time is linear, progress does not have to be. Times of enhanced objectivity offer us the lens through which we can view reality, and realign our priorities with a more accurate sense of what is important. Hazy, illusory options are replaced by clearly lit paths. Our ego is temporarily blinded, and we have the ability to jump

---

35. The *Maharal* teaches that since the spiritual world is beyond time, the quicker we advance towards the process, the less physicality sticks to us, and the more spiritual or Divine assistance we receive.

forward. This is how we tip the balance of free will . . .
if, and only *if* . . . we choose to take action in that defin-
ing moment.[36]

36. Chazal say, "Everything goes after the beginning." This is why
people are very careful in their behavior on Rosh Hashanah (the
Jewish New Year), so that their entire year will reflect their intentions
at this time.

SECTION

II

RISING ABOVE
OUR NATURE

CHAPTER 4

THE POWER OF SELF-ACCEPTANCE

"The very seal of God is Truth."
—Talmud, Shabbat 55a

When reality clashes with our ability to accept it, it creates an internal conflict called *cognitive dissonance*. Under this psychological weight, those who have low self-esteem feel the need to justify themselves. They have to make sense of their world and choices in the least painful way, where *being right* becomes more of an emotional priority than *doing what is right*.[37]

---

37. The Gemara (*Sanhedrin* 105a) recounts a dialogue between the Jews and the Prophets, in which the Jews attempted to rationalize and create excuses for their lack of commitment to God. They claimed that (1) since God sent them into exile, they owe Him nothing. "Does a servant who is sold by his master owe any allegiance to him? Likewise, does a wife whose husband divorces her owe him anything?" and (2) they can't repent for the evil inclination that rules over them. *Yad Ramah* explains that the Jews were purely looking for excuses to rationalize their unwillingness to repent.

In fact, we all do this to varying degrees, because just as human beings have a body, we also have an ego. Self-esteem, therefore, is not an all-or-nothing proposition; rather, it runs along a spectrum with many shades of gray.

To illustrate, imagine that you buy a watch for $500. Afterwards, you flip through a magazine and see what appears to be the same watch, but advertised for $300. This discovery produces an emotional inconsistency. We want to see ourselves as smart consumers and savvy shoppers, but the advertisement appears to provide evidence to the contrary. Either we were duped and overpaid, or the advertisement does not represent what appears to be the truth. Our level of self-esteem determines our thought process. If we have a healthy level of self-esteem, we will take note of the advertisement and, if we believe it to be accurate, will conclude that we made a mistake.

When we lack self-esteem, we are often unable to look at ourselves as the cause of the problem, because we cannot afford to be wrong emotionally.[38] Instead of conceding that we erred, we prefer to believe that "The world is unfair," or "People are crooked." Thus,

---

38. ". . . but they did not recognize him" (Genesis 42:8). Joseph the Righteous' brothers were mere feet away from him, yet they could not see reality. The brothers simply could not fathom that they were wrong for all those years. They stared at reality, yet their egos would not let them see.

the seedlings of neuroses and paranoia take root. Before
our conscious mind is forced to accept an unpleasant
reality, we may also realign values and decide quickly
that time is more important than money, and that it's
simply not worthwhile to shop for lower prices. Either
way, something has to give.[39]

Our instincts protect our psychological wellbeing in
much the same way as we protect our physical bodies.
When our physical welfare is threatened, a natural fight-
or-flight response is engaged. Similarly, when our psychological wellbeing is threatened, we engage our
accept-or-deflect response. When a mind is healthy and
strong, a challenge to the self is usually accepted and
confronted directly. A mind that is not strong may
instead deflect the threat.[40]

Just as a physically weak person will shy away from
physical challenges, deflection becomes a conditioned
response for the psychologically weak. A person who is
emotionally unwell reacts to conflicts in the following
ways: "You are wrong," or "This is just how I am." There

39. While most people with low self-esteem will refuse to accept responsibility, those with even more extreme low self-esteem may beat themselves up and become angry and annoyed with themselves. Healthy
self-esteem allows a person to recognize his mistakes, without condemn-
ing himself OR the world.
40. "All of man's ways are pure in his own eyes" (Proverbs 16:2). Rashi
and Metzudot explain that one doesn't wish to find fault with oneself.

is little room for, "I was wrong," the acknowledgment of personal responsibility. Such a person deflects the world and his own insecurities and, in the process, grows weaker, because the psychological self can only develop through acceptance. This is our emotional immune system. In the person who lacks self-esteem, the deflection response engages at all times. Everything is considered a threat to his psychological security.[41]

Every time we refuse to acknowledge the truth about any aspect of ourselves (or condemn ourselves for being imperfect), we send the unconscious message, "I am inadequate." As an analogy, today's vehicles are designed so that in an accident, the vehicle absorbs as much of the collision's energy as possible. This absorbed energy cannot be recovered, since it goes into the permanent deformation of the vehicle. In the same way, when we collide with reality and refuse to accept it, we get dented.

Denying the truth does not make it go away. It makes us—the real us—go away. If we are completely honest with ourselves (and by extension, with others), then the ego does not engage.[42] It only survives and thrives in a world of falsehood.

34

41. Consider the four stages of grief: denial, anger, depression, and acceptance. The first three stages are ego-based. It is only when the ego's influences are removed that a person moves to acceptance.
42. "The Lord God is truth" (Jeremiah 10:10). "Keep far away from anything false" (Exodus 23:7).

Once we have fully accepted something about ourselves or our lives, we no longer need to hide from it. We don't care who knows about it or who finds out, and we don't allow the reality to hold us back. At this point, our fears dissolve, because there is no longer a threat of exposing ourselves. The only thing that can ever be rejected is an image. [43] The truth, once embraced, can never be bruised or injured, yet a delusion can be shattered by a whisper or a glance.

There is nothing wrong in seeing ourselves as less than perfect; it is honest and healthy. This is a far cry from the person who sees his imperfections and then condemns himself as worthless or lacking.

43. Public speaking is typically ranked as the number one fear. Death is ranked at number two. To eliminate jitters associated with public speaking, one only needs to focus on making the audience feel good about themselves. When we decide that everything we say and do is out of compassion for them, a step in the direction of giving, we cannot feel anxiety. Public speaking is a universal fear, and it is significantly diminished by changing our focus. It is interesting to note that the greater the difference between the image we wish to project and our true self, the greater the fear. This is why those who do not care to impress anyone will not be nervous; they are not projecting an image. This is true in other aspects of life as well: the closer our true self is to the image we want others to see, the less fear we have. Of course, our image is projected by the ego, which is why the less ego we have, the more secure and calm we become. Any time we deviate from reality, we move into unstable territory.

A Window or a Mirror

Nature is designed to reveal God's presence for those who learn to see; at the same time, nature blocks God's presence for those who cannot see beyond themselves. This is precisely why God only shows us reality, but does not give us a greater degree of clarity.[44] Unless we can accept ourselves, we cannot see past ourselves. We are too busy judging, blaming, and distorting our world.

Each moment of every day carries the potential for gaining perspective—whether through observing a leaf fall from a tree or appreciating the wonders of the human body. Regrettably, we frequently ignore what is in front of our very eyes, and thus most of us only gain perspective through significant life experiences or extraordinary world events; and the more self-absorbed we are, the greater the experience needs to be in order to budge our attention away from ourselves.

---

44. At Mount Sinai, approximately 2.5 to 3 million Jews experienced mass prophecy, in the form of a direct revelation from God, as well as receiving the Ten Commandments from Him. This prophecy was temporary and short-lived, because it was external rather than acquired through personal growth.

CHAPTER 5

THE FIRST CAUSE

*"And God created the man in his
own image . . ."*
—GENESIS 1:27

The process of growth appears to be a *closed system*, in which every component depends on the previous one to exist, and progression or regression moves incrementally. To summarize: our ability to maintain self-control helps us to make better choices. Consequently, our self-esteem is increased, which automatically deflates the ego. A smaller ego, of course, means greater perspective. Greater perspective, in turn, makes it easier for us to maintain self-control, and so the process moves forward or backwards, depending on our willpower to rise above our nature and make good choices.

Enhanced emotional health can be achieved by bypassing this measured process, and moving past this closed circuit. Beyond taking immediate action when we are inspired by flashes of perspective, being able to *accept ourselves completely* organically purges the ego, which automatically taps us into an undistorted reality. Once we do this, then our eyes would perceive a different reality; we would see truth . . . God . . . reality, everywhere.

GAINING COMPLETE SELF-ACCEPTANCE

When we look to creation itself, we find that there has to be a first Cause—and we know this Cause to be God.[45] We can have creations (living beings, animate and inanimate forces, and objects) that were created by other entities, but as we go back in time, we discover that something outside of this closed system had to have been responsible for setting things in motion. We cannot have everything depending on something else—some force had to be independent. God is that independent force which "began" our universe.

Since we are created in the image of the Creator, there must be a first cause *within* us but, at the same time, *beyond* us. There must be a way to move forward that is "outside of the circle" whenever we choose. So what can we, as finite beings, bring to life that is completely independent of ourselves?

45. *Rambam* (*Hilchot Yesodei HaTorah* 1:1).

Our own first cause is the *recognition* that we are independent. The Sages state, "How precious is man for he was created in the image of God."[46] The God-given gift of free will bestowed upon all human beings, however, is secondary to the Divine gift of awareness. As the Talmud says, "A greater sign of our preciousness to God is that He *told* us we were created in the image of God."[47]

God, being non-physical, does not have a form, so what do we mean when we speak of man being created in the image of God? It means that human beings have the freedom to forge their own reality. In that way we resemble God, Who is completely free and independent.[48]

Free will gives human beings the ability to rise above their nature.[49] This gift was not bestowed on any other creature, as illustrated in the classic Aesop's fable about the turtle and the scorpion.

39

---

46. "And God said, 'Let us make man in our image, after our likeness' . . . and God created the man in his own image, and in the image of God He created him" (Genesis 1:26, 27).

47. Ethics of the Fathers 3:18.

48. That man resembles God, in having free will, is the interpretation according to the Rambam (*Yad, Teshuvah* 5:1) and many other commentators.

49. "All of God's service depends on the improvement of one character. Character traits are fundamental to the performance of mitzvot and to Torah principles. Conversely, all sins stem from unimproved character traits" (Vilna Gaon, *Even Shleimah* 1:1).

"Would you help me cross the river?" the scorpion asked the turtle. "Jump on!" says the turtle, "but you have to promise not to sting me." "I promise," the scorpion says, emphatically. He then jumps on. The turtle swims across the river. Just as they get to the other bank, the scorpion stings the turtle. "Why did you sting me?" asks the turtle painfully as he takes his last breath and sinks under the water. "I had to," the scorpion answers.

Animals are incapable of repressing their urges and exercising self-control. Their actions reflect their desires. When we, however, as human beings, utilize our free will, we become partners in our own creation.[50] That is why it is said that the purpose of creation rests on free will.[51]

50. At the beginning of creation, God gave us life. He is a Giver, while human beings are, by nature, takers. Only by applying free will, through which we choose to give instead of take, do we move closer to Him. According to the Talmud and the *Shulchan Aruch*, a Jew is required to say one hundred blessings a day, beginning with the complex and beautiful wonder that our life is renewed each morning. This helps to foster the mentality that moves one from a taker (of food and of life) to a giver (of thanks).

51. *Derech HaShem* (1:2:1). We said earlier, that when we gain perspective we find that previously bothersome circumstances become irrelevant. We also stated that perspective allows us to appreciate what we have, spawning feelings of gratitude and humility. These two themes come together because we find at the zenith of perspective, the only

As long as we believe that the quality of our lives is a result of circumstances, rather than a result of our own proactive choices and response to situations, we remain powerless.[52] All positive change begins with some version of, "I am responsible and nothing in my life will change for the better unless I change."[53] This is not meant to be an affirmation or mantra to be repeated; rather, once we affirm this insight as truth, it is forever a part of us.

Why is acceptance of responsibility the path to self-acceptance? We take responsibility for that which we accept, and we ignore that which we do not want to see. Nothing in nature is irrelevant; everything has a purpose. Our life, and everything in it, must be acknowledged. When we ignore something, anything, no matter how insignificant, we move into the world of falsehood

41

---

thing that matters, is the one thing that we can truly call our own: *free will*. With it, we choose our reality; and that is all that is relevant.

52. "If I am not for myself, who will be for me?" (Ethics of the Fathers 1:14). In reference to this saying: "If I don't take responsibility and commit to personal growth, who will do it for me?" (*Rambam, Rabbeinu Yonah*).

53. If you were to witness a vehicular accident, would you do something? Bystander apathy is the term given to a lack of impetus for individuals to help when there are others present. This is because responsibility is diffused as each person feels that someone else will help. In fact, studies show that, as the number of witnesses of an incident increases, individuals' response time actually decreases.

and, by default, suffering.[54] Acceptance of responsibility instantly leads to a wider perspective, as we allow more reality into our view. We have no interest in denying what is necessary to our wellbeing—for certain, we strive to see clearly. The recently diagnosed diabetic, for instance, is likely to analyze every type of food in his diet. Blaming bad genes, his parents, and a hectic lifestyle fades into insignificance. His focus moves away from what is unproductive.

In the Beginning

When he was created, Adam Harishon (the first man) had complete perspective, as the ego was external. As a result of the sin, however, the ego became part of our internal composition.[55] Adam and Eve are told by God

54. Applied kinesiology demonstrates that our body is highly attuned to that which is unhealthy or false. For instance, one interesting test shows the effects of various substances on the human body. If a person were to hold his arm in front of his body, he would resist having the arm pushed down. However, once this person places a small sample of an injurious substance in his hand, the ability for his arm to maintain the same levels of strength is often significantly diminished. (Note: issues of efficacy and *avoda zara* may exist.)

55. By removing the ego, the capacity for prophecy is theoretically restored. With the explanation of the Sefer Hasidim and the Vilna Gaon that the disappearance of prophecy is linked to the eradication of idolatry, the prevalence of self-worship via the ego replaces idolatry or outside worship.

that they can eat freely and enjoy everything in the Garden of Eden. They just cannot eat from the Tree of Knowledge of Good and Bad. As we know, a serpent entices Eve to eat fruit from this tree. After she eats from the tree, she gives some of its fruit to Adam. When God confronts Adam and Eve about their actions, "[t]he man said, 'The woman whom you gave to be with me—she gave me of the tree, and I ate.' The woman said, 'The serpent deceived me, and I ate.'"[56]

The Midrash says that God asks Adam, *ayeka* ("Where are you?"), to give Adam an opportunity to confess his sin and repent before God speaks again and pronounces punishment. Instead of accepting responsibility, Adam blames his sin on Eve, and Eve blames the snake. Had they acknowledged the wrong, they would have been more readily forgiven. *When we accept responsibility for our actions and our lives, we purge ourselves of our ego.*[57]

56. Genesis 3:8–13.

57. It is not practical to control every detail of our being, but we should not feel free to disregard them, either. Our physical wellbeing, for instance, cannot be ignored, but we do not need to make our weight an all-consuming focus. Rather, if we choose to move these matters to the periphery of our lives, then we should simply be aware that we need to take good care, and begin to move in the right direction, even if we start by eating one less cookie a week. Of course, this has almost zero effect on our health. Making a conscious decision, however, to pay attention to our physical wellbeing is the real objective.

Each situation brings with it the opportunity to excuse our behavior or to take responsibility. It is correct to say, "I am doing this because I cannot control myself," instead of saying, "This is right." The first statement is truthful. The second is a lie.

This cannot be stressed enough. Even when we choose to *not* take responsibility for our actions, as long as we *recognize* that we *could* have behaved differently, our intellectual awareness is raised to a much higher level. This approach stands in contrast to the feeling of being out of control, and perceiving oneself to be a victim of circumstance. Rather than justifying our actions, it is preferable to acknowledge that we have chosen not to act responsibly.[58] By reminding ourselves that we always have a choice, we reinforce the notion that we are responsible, whether or not we ultimately act responsibly. Instead of burying our choices behind the illusion of helplessness, we are facing reality.[59]

---

58. *Cheshbon Hanefesh* is a spiritual accounting. It is important to examine our day, to see where we exceeded our goals, and where we may have fallen short. This should not be done in a judgmental way; rather, it should be done with the same kindness that we would show a loved one.
59. In *Reality Therapy*, Dr. William Glasser writes, "In their unsuccessful effort to fulfill their needs, no matter what behavior they choose, all patients have a common characteristic: they all deny the reality of the world around them . . . Whether it is a partial denial or the total blotting out of all of reality of the chronic backward patient in the state hospital, the denial of some or all of reality is common to patients.

LIVING IN THE WORLD OF TRUTH

Embracing the *knowledge* that we are responsible for our actions eventually prompts our soul to *act* more responsibly, and therefore transform ourselves. We can further advance this process by making it easier to rise above our nature. The first criterion for doing this is that we move our lives in the direction of our soul's longing, rather than reactively going through life with an ego-oriented agenda. Only when we are dissatisfied with the general direction of our lives do we allow the petty annoyances to blow out of proportion, causing us significant stress. In the next chapter we will see how this movement is properly achieved.

45

The second criterion is to recognize the effect of our actions. A person, for example, may have a difficult time resisting a favorite unhealthy food, and is only occasionally able to tap into his inner wellspring of discipline. If, however, he develops a life-threatening allergy to this particular food, then his ability to resist is made a great deal easier. Did he suddenly get a boost of self-esteem or willpower? No. The stakes have changed.

Therapy will be successful when they are able to give up denying the world and recognize that reality exists but that they must fulfill their needs within its framework" (Glasser, W. *Reality Therapy*. Harper & Row. 1965).

Certainly, as we increase self-esteem, we will want to invest in our wellbeing and long-term satisfaction and happiness. Irrespective of our feelings of self-worth, when the cost is just not worth it, we are forced to re-evaluate the situation. From our example we find that even without a change in ourselves, we are driven to change our behavior when we connect completely, to the impact and influence that our actions have on the entirety of our wellbeing.

The job of the ego is to cloak reality, and to hide from us, those consequences. Once we understand the inner workings of human nature, we lift that veil. Then, when a choice presents itself, we will appreciate clearly, what is to be gained, and what is to be lost.[60]

60. "Open my eyes and I will see wondrous things from your Torah" (Psalms119:18).

CHAPTER 6

LIVING YOUR LIFE

*"If you are not going upward then you are
automatically falling downward."*
—CHAZAL

The *pinnacle* of personal responsibility is to *take our lives
seriously.* When we do not devote the time and attention
to working out how we can achieve our goals, we are
sending a message to our unconscious that it does not
matter how we live. The psychological damage that is
caused as a result of such a casual attitude is inevitable.

Diligent pursuit of our ambitions consists of five
main components: having *meaningful* objectives, design-
ing a realistic plan for achieving them, creating a proper
structure, setting deadlines (where necessary), and moving forward with complete honesty and integrity.

What do *You* Want?

There is no status quo in nature.[61] The law of conservation states that organisms die if they do not grow. Moreover, just as every person is one of a kind—from their fingerprints, to their face, to their DNA—we similarly are all born with a specific purpose that is unique to us.[62]

In order to obtain the highest level of fulfillment—self-actualization[63]—we must be moving towards that

61. "The path of life is to rise for the intelligent one, lest he fall to the lowest depths" (Proverbs 15: 24). The Vilna Gaon explains that a person doesn't remain standing: he is either going up or down. We must therefore move upward, for by remaining static, we are automatically moving downward. Human beings are wired by God to feel pleasure when we are productive. This is why, incongruously, the person who is most often frustrated in slow-moving traffic is the one who is going nowhere fast in life.

62. When we are busy building an image or giving in to cravings and impulses, we never rise above reactionary living. We respond to life, but we do not live it, and so we become easily depressed. We are driven to express our creativity and individuality. "Just as our faces are all different, so are their ideas never the same" (Sanhedrin 38a).

63. Abraham Maslow's "hierarchy of needs" behavioral model distinguishes between two types of needs: 1) deficiency needs, such as hunger and thirst, or the need for security, which can be satisfied by providing adequate amounts of food, drink, or safety; and 2) growth needs, such as the need for learning and self-actualization, which can only be satisfied by continuing development. The apex of self-actualization is obtained to the extent that our objectives are altruistic, because the logical conclusion to our ongoing development is to be a giver, like God.

which our soul desires. The soul is a "spark" of the Divine essence, so when we actualize our God-given potential, we attach ourselves to the most stable force possible. Living in a way that is inconsistent, or opposite to our true selves is not only unfulfilling, it is exhausting.[64] If we do not have a clear vision of what we want out of our lives, then we are moving through life reactively; we never realize the full force of our free will, which is to proactively move our lives in the direction of our choosing.[65]

Too often, we confine our options to a small space, not fully recognizing the range of possibilities that extend beyond our comfort zone. Our egos lead us to believe that we are boxed in, and cannot go beyond where we are, or can only move a little, slowly. Lack of inspiration is really lack of enthusiasm for the direction in which we believe we can move.

49

---

64. Rav Shneur Kotler (*Noam Siach* Vol. 1 p. 195) expounds on how disconnecting from one's source leads to tiredness and lackadaisical work.

65. "Remember the Sabbath, to keep it holy. Six days you shall labor, and do all your work; but the seventh day is a Sabbath unto the Lord Your God, in it you shall not do any manner of work . . ." (Exodus 20:8–11). The concept of Shabbat, the crown of creation, and the day of rest, cannot exist without the concept of work. Moreover, a person who spends his life working has a greater appreciation for retirement than one who has not been seriously engaged in such work. To him all of the days feel alike; there is no separation.

To become reenergized, we need to expand our thinking and to ask the right question instead of looking at the same problem. Saying, "I hate my life," does not produce an answer that moves us forward. It is not even a question, but a statement that reinforces complacency. We must open ourselves up to the field of possibilities by asking ourselves, "What do I want out of life?"

CHECK YOUR MOTIVATION

We must be honest about *why* we want what we want. So many people are miserable because they set goals based on someone else's expectations. They had every reason for doing what they did, except for the right reason—because it was important to them, for their own growth, and for creating the future they truly wanted.

If any of our objectives hinge on outside approval or acceptance, we will never be independent, and we will always look to the rest of the world for emotional reinforcement.

The accepted, collective, distortion of accomplishment seeps into almost every area of our lives. How might we define the following traits: wisdom, strength, wealth, and honor? Typically, wisdom is characterized by the scope of our knowledge; strength by the extent that we can control and dominate other people or situations; wealth by the possessions we have amassed; and honor by the degree and type of positive recognition that we have received.

Note that these are all ego-oriented definitions, whereas success and failure are functions of contrast and comparison. The Torah not only espouses the importance of these sought-after traits, but it also clarifies the correct path to attain them. "Who is wise? The one who learns from others. Who is strong? The one who controls his emotions. Who is rich? The one who is happy with his lot. Who is honored? The one who honors others."[66] The acquisition of these traits is not competitively based. We cannot achieve personal growth and raise our self-esteem, merely by showing up and doing better than someone else. And yet, outrageously so, our culture not only reinforces this mentality, we celebrate it.

The Olympics have three medal places: gold, silver, and bronze. This means that the fourth-place finisher is a loser. In fact, one study shows that, on average, the bronze medalist appears happier than the silver medalist. The research concludes that the athletes' emotional response is driven by comparison with the most easily imagined alternative. Silver medalists are preoccupied with having lost the gold, while bronze medalists are overjoyed to have won a medal instead of walking away with nothing.[67]

51

---

66. Ethics of the Fathers 4:1.
67. Medvec, V. H., Madey, S. F., & Gilovich, T. (1995). "When less is

This idea of accomplishment—a system that is doomed to fail—is defined by an egocentric mindset that forces us to become dependent on others in order to feel successful. This is sheer insanity, and a recipe for mental instability.

Ever more subtle, a corrupted understanding of self-esteem leads us to believe the equation: self-esteem = self-respect + self-efficacy (the ability to be effective with our choices). According to this model, we can try our very best to do what is right, but in the end, if things do not turn out as expected or hoped (i.e., if we are not effective), then we will not gain self-esteem. We may feel this to be true in our own lives. If we try to do something kind for another person, but our efforts backfire and we cause the person more difficulty, then we do not necessarily walk away from the experience feeling better about ourselves.

On investigation, we find the ego lurking behind this muddled thinking. The ego is outcome-oriented.[68] It wants results of which it can feel proud and requires evidence that it is effective with a tangible, visible payoff.

_____

more: Counterfactual thinking and satisfaction among Olympic medalists." *Journal of Personality and Social Psychology,* 69, 603–610.

68. While we should not be consumed with outcomes, we should adjust our approach if we are unsuccessful in order to produce what we believe to be right.

In the physical world, cause and effect are correlated, though separate entities. An action produces a result. In the non-physical world, where free will exists, cause and effect must be simultaneous, as there is actually no time or space. Therefore, efficacy is achieved by the mere act of choosing to move in a meaningful direction.[69] In other words, self-respect translates directly into self-esteem.[70]

A Galvanized Soul

An objective that neutralizes the ego helps us to develop the flexibility that not only brings us emotional stability, but also allows us to effortlessly direct our attention.[71] An athlete or artist who is "in the zone" is flawless in his performance. He is neither self-aware nor self-conscious.[72]

53

---

69. Michtav Me'eliyahu (Vol. 1, p. 115; Kuntres Habechirah Ch. 4).
70. "If you make the effort, you will find results" (*Megillah* 6b). Pleasure is inherent in the *pursuit* of a meaningful objective, and God will bring forth from our efforts, an outcome that is good for us, whether or not progress is apparent.
71. While it is not possible to remove every last trace of ego from our motivation, we must strive to make our pursuit as genuine and as pure as possible.
72. The Alter of Slabodka explains that Jacob was able to lift the rock off the well when he saw Rachel approaching, something that all the shepherds had to do together, because he focused all of his energies in order to help her. His singular concentration allowed him to accomplish this superhuman feat.

When we are engaged in this way, we can forget that we haven't eaten or slept in some time, because we are divorced from the influence of the physical.[73] Someone who can spend hours on his favorite hobby loses track of time, because of the intense concentration on his objective and not on himself.[74] Even though it is isolating, he is not bored because he is not truly alone. When what we are doing is an act of love, we feel little or no pain.[75]

In addition, we go after what we want without the reigns of self-doubt because when it is not about us, we can access any trait that we need in order to accomplish what we wish. Imagine a mother who loses sight of her child on a busy sidewalk. Does she care what anyone thinks of her as she frantically yells out her child's name? She will do whatever is necessary to find her child, and therefore engages in behaviors outside the scope of her

73. God revealed himself to Moses at such a high level of revelation that Moses' body became purified and his soul was able to emanate through it. These are the "rays of glory" which the Torah mentions Moses exuding (Exodus 34:29), and that is why he no longer needed to eat or drink to sustain himself for the 40 days he spent in heaven; he had received his sustenance directly from God, and not through physical means (Exodus 34:28).

74. Einstein's famous theory of relativity (E=mc2) illustrates just this idea. To paraphrase, "When a man sits with his beloved wife for an hour, it seems like only a minute. But let him sit on a hot stove for a minute and it's longer than any hour."

75. "Jacob worked for seven years for Rachel, and they seemed to him as a few days, because of his love for her" (Genesis 29:20).

typical personality. Her thoughts are occupied with her one objective—to find her child.

A Plan of Action

Beyond choosing the direction, we also need a plan for how to get there. Not many people would go to the airport, and get on a plane that takes them to just any sunny destination. We typically plan our trips by booking flights, arranging for transportation to the hotel, perhaps even planning an itinerary so that we know exactly what we hope to accomplish. Similarly, it is irresponsible for us to have a general idea of our goals in life, without a specific plan of how to achieve them.

55

While many factors go into effective planning, none injure our success more than when we abandon a straight path in favor of a convoluted plan that needlessly complicates our pursuit. *Occam's razor*, a principle attributed to a fourteenth-century logician, states that, "Entities should not be multiplied unnecessarily." Or put more plainly, if you have two equally likely solutions to a problem, pick the simplest. A circuitous route borne out of fear of failure, fear or success, or both, and is one of the ego's favorite tools. It tricks us into feeling like we are moving forward, when in actuality, we are going around in circles.

Setting a Realistic Time Frame

We do not run the universe, but we do run our lives. Establishing a timetable does *not* mean that we should expect specific quantifiable results, but we need a time frame in which to operate.[76] It is instinctive to wait until conditions become more favorable, or until we have more information, or until we are in a better mood before taking an action. Society operates on deadlines and expiration dates because if there is no immediate need to move forward, then most people will not do so.[77] If we do not set a realistic schedule for our objectives (where appropriate), we are not only making a mockery out of our lives, but we are working against the laws of human nature.

Parkinson's Law states that, "Work expands to fill the time available." He expounds on this law with, "General recognition of this fact is shown in the proverbial phrase,

---

76. "Teach us to count our days properly, so that we may bring wisdom to our hearts" (*Tehillim* 90:12). The Chofetz Chaim states that the most people manage their lives like a person on vacation writing to his friend on a picture postcard. By the time he finishes with the introduction and usual pleasantries, he sorrowfully realizes that he has no more room left to write what he really wanted to say.

77. This principle of human nature accounts for the "beat-the-clock" scenario that seems to unfold before every Shabbat. Even when Shabbat begins later, we often find ourselves in that same frantic rush as we do when sundown is a couple of hours earlier. With "so much extra time," our activities expand until Shabbat comes in.

'It is the busiest man who has time to spare,'" and follows with this amusing anecdote:

> Thus, an elderly lady of leisure can spend the entire day in writing and dispatching a postcard to her niece at Bognor Regis. An hour will be spent finding the postcard, another in hunting for spectacles, half an hour in a search for the address, an hour and a quarter in composition, and twenty minutes in deciding whether or not to take an umbrella when going to the pillar box in the next street. The total effort that would occupy a busy man for three minutes all told may in this fashion leave another person prostrate after a day of doubt, anxiety, and toil. Granted that work (and especially paperwork) is thus elastic in its demands on time, it is manifest that there need be little or no relationship between the work to be done and the size of the staff to which it may be assigned. A lack of real activity does not, of necessity, result in leisure. A lack of occupation is not necessarily revealed by a manifest idleness. The thing to be done swells in importance and complexity in a direct ratio with the time to be spent.[78]

57

---

78. C. Northcote Parkinson, *Parkinson's Law: The Pursuit of Progress*, London, John Murray (1958). Cyril Northcote Parkinson (1909–1993) was a scholar in the fields of public administration and time management.

Without a timetable, minutia takes over our lives, and inflates to levels of unproductive importance.

Stability Within Structure

When we create structure in our lives, we allow for growth.[79] Without it, our energy dissipates. Structure helps us to move in a meaningful, productive direction, and helps prevent us from succumbing to passing whims and desires.[80]

Imagine being let loose in a jewelry store for a five-minute shopping spree. Unless we have an idea in our minds of what we want to buy, we will gravitate towards any shiny piece of jewelry that catches our eye. Lack of structure does not free us; it paralyzes us.[81]

Virtually every religion dictates a code of conduct. There are things that are permitted and things that are forbidden. Although we may agree or disagree with the specifics, such boundaries and borders are necessary to

58

79. Pruning is a process of directing growth—that is, energy—in the way you want it to go. Every living entity has limited resources, so cutting away and eliminating what you do not want allows for greater utilization of the existing energy.
80. It is said that the Alter of Kelm once went to visit his son in his yeshiva. He went to his son's room and checked his drawers. He saw that they were in order and he said he saw enough to know that his son is doing OK. "If his drawers are in order, then his head is in order."
81. Rav Shneur Kotler (*Noam Siach* Vol. 1, p. 195).

our emotional health.[82] Someone who does not feel in control needs, most of all, a sense of structure. Aptly, the Hebrew prayer book is called the Siddur, which means "order."[83]

Structure helps to simplify, harmonize, and synchronize our thoughts and lives. For instance, if family is important to us—as it should be, according to the Torah—then we should not simply fit our family commitments into our day; rather, we should design our day around those commitments.[84] When we establish our priorities, we should make sure we allocate sufficient time for them.[85]

59

ACTING WITH INTEGRITY

Lack of integrity saps our energy. It is like having one foot on the gas and the other on the brake. We burn out.

82. "One who learns without structure cannot acquire wisdom. His learning is mixed up in his mind, and nothing is retained with clarity" (*Ramchal, Sefer Havikuach*, p. 76).
83. The word "Halacha" comes from the word "haloch," which means "to go." Halacha, the code of Jewish Law, gives us the structure through which we can move ahead in our path of life.
84. The flipside of this rule is equally compelling. Having the courage to move in the right direction requires us to have the fortitude to close the door on that which is no longer productive and constructive.
85. "Make your Torah study a fixed practice" (Ethics of the Fathers 1:15).

Newton's first law of motion speaks to the tendency of a body in motion to stay in motion, due to the property of inertia. What slows it down is friction; what slows *us* down is dishonesty. We must be as truthful as possible with ourselves and others about our motivations, intentions, and actions.[86] Whether it is keeping our word or conducting ourselves ethically, we must not think that the Creator of the universe will allow us to gain in any way from being untruthful.

In spite of the short-term gain that seems so real, does it make sense that God will allow us to benefit by using deception? On the contrary, such actions breed arrogance and impede our ability to succeed. Imagine a person who steals $100. He puts the money in his pocket and then he takes it out and looks at it. He can feel it, he can smell it, and he can see it. He can even spend it. Can we say, though, that he is $100 richer? Will he derive any benefit from that $100 because he stole it? No.

Let us appreciate the finer implication here. The extent of our determination to properly living our lives reflects the influx of Divine assistance. [87] When a person,

---

86. The Torah allows for deception in limited instances, when it comes to sparing one from embarrassment, for example. The intricacies of the exemptions are beyond the scope of this work.

87. To the degree that a person has trust, God helps him. We see this in the story of the spies (Numbers 13:1) who were sent out to report on

in spite of what appears to him to be a loss or a setback, conducts himself with the highest degree of integrity, he demonstrates his trust in God and gains the support of the universe.[88] If our principles become compromised, not only do we sever access to the Infinite, but we lose respect for ourselves, and once again become dependent, and by extension, frustrated by any lack of ego-satiating, real-world progress.

Tomorrow Will Never Come

If we tell ourselves that we want to live more responsibly, but that it is better to wait until things "calm down a bit," we are deluding ourselves . . . because we have it backwards.

61

the land and did not fully acknowledge that their ability to secure the land was not based on military might, but on God's will. Their lack of trust is what made it impossible to conquer the land: since they believed that it was entirely up to them, this fundamental lack of trust would lead to their defeat.

88. "The man (Ya'akov) became exceedingly prosperous" (Genesis 30:43). Rambam (*Hilchos Sechirus* 13:7) writes: "The same way an employee is obligated not to cheat his impoverished worker or to hold back his wages, so too is the worker obligated not to cheat his employer by wasting time from work here and there. He must be exceedingly careful to work his full allotted time . . . and must labor with all his energy, as we find that Ya'akov the *tzadik* said to his wives, 'Now you have known that I served your father with all of my might' (Genesis 31:6). Due to his impeccable honesty he received his reward in this world . . ."

When something does not act in accordance with its purpose, it can only bring dysfunction and pain. The very reason for life's bumps, twists, and turns is to help us direct our lives in a meaningful way. Our struggles are like the guardrail on a narrow, windy, cliff. A driver would not say, "As soon as I stop banging into these barriers, then I will be free to move forward." He, of course, recognizes that the scratches and dents are much better than the alternative—going off the cliff entirely.

Life's travails exist in order to wake us up, to get us moving in the right direction. This is why they will never cease, because even when we are on the right path, we will always need to make minor course corrections along the way.[89] In the next chapter we'll see how these course corrections, while painful, do not cause us to suffer when we are living our lives with meaning.

---

89. A plane is off-course during about 90% of a flight. However, the pilot or automatic pilot is constantly making adjustments to bring the plane back on course. Consequently, the plane reaches its destination even though it was off-course for most of the flight.

SECTION

III

EMOTIONAL
FREEDOM

CHAPTER 7

REALITY WILL NEVER GO AWAY

*"Everything has its season, and there is a
time for everything under the heaven."*
—ECCLESIASTES 3:1

In today's world, modern conveniences and technology
have made our lives easier, but they have also made us
complacent. In previous generations, life was consider-
ably more difficult, and intense labor was the norm.[90]
Today, if the chair is not comfy, replace it with another
one. If it's too hot, turn on the air conditioning. If you
have a headache, take a pill.

---

90. Rabbi Yaakov Tzvi Mecklenburg states in *Haktav v'hakabbalah* that
one of the reasons that the Jews were subjected to the perils of Egyptian
exile is that they would not have otherwise been willing to accept the
Torah with its many obligations and restrictions. In short, the notion
that life can often be difficult needed to be instilled in their psyche so
that they would be shaken out of their complacency.

As life becomes increasingly more comfortable, we are falling out of the habit of exerting ourselves, and have gotten used to the idea that comfort is the path to happiness. (Or perhaps more damaging is the notion that comfort *is* happiness.) It therefore stands to reason that the idea of sacrificing our creature comforts in order to pursue our goals and desires has become foreign. In our minds, life should be easy.

Lying on the couch and watching TV is undoubtedly comfortable, but hardly meaningful, and so, by definition, offers little, if any, lasting pleasure.[91] To be more precise, the feeling is not really pleasure at all, but mere comfort, which is the avoidance of pain. If we seek to avoid pain, then we are, in essence, avoiding life.

But there is no escape! If we spend our lives avoiding effort, we cannot move forward and thus rather than avoiding suffering, we end up experiencing more of it. Accepting responsibility is paradoxically the easiest way

91. How can we be afraid of something that happens to a character on a television show we're watching? We know the show is not real, and we may even know what's going to happen, yet we suspend our intellect and allow ourselves to become absorbed in the illusion. The more we are engaged in life, the less enjoyment we find in such pursuits because we cannot escape our intellect as easily. We are grounded in the real world. On the other hand, someone who is prone to indulging himself in escapism easily suspends his intellect, as this is what he does during his "real" life.

through life—because we maximize pleasure and mini-
mize pain. Like most things worthwhile, it's only hard in
the beginning, and then we reap the rewards.

Whenever we take responsibility for ourselves and
our lives, and do something productive—no matter how
minor—we feel better.[92] People who join a gym, for
instance, suddenly find themselves to be in an unusually
good mood, even before they have lifted a single weight
or swum a single lap. Why? Because they have sent a
message to their unconscious that said, "I am making an
investment in myself."[93]

The more engaged we are in life and the pursuit of
meaningful goals, the greater our pleasure and ultimate
sense of satisfaction.[94] Do we really want to live superficial

92. When we live only for today, we send a message to our unconscious
that says, "I don't care what happens to me tomorrow." This harms us
emotionally. From a psychological perspective, the mere act of treating
ourselves better makes us like ourselves more. The fundamental law that
governs this phenomenon is the aforementioned concept of cognitive
dissonance. By taking a specific action that says, "I like myself enough
to put time and energy into who I am," we imbue ourselves with a
greater sense of self-worth.
93. In order to orient itself, our unconscious mind often takes its cues
from our conscious behavior. Studies have also shown that the mere act
of smiling makes us feel better. Smiling releases endorphins, natural pain
killers, and serotonin. In fact, research shows that smiling is often
accompanied by a measurable reduction in blood pressure.
94. King Solomon stated: ". . . he who increases knowledge increases
pain" (Ecclesiastes 1:18). On the surface, this does not seem like a

lives that are comfortable, yet lack meaning? Having fun and acquiring material comforts are not enough; our soul gnaws at us to do more, to become more.

A mother may say that as long as her child is happy, she does not care what the child does, but this is not really so. If the "child" is 40 years old and plays video games all day instead of earning a living, the mother will not be pleased . . . and this 40-year-old child cannot experience real pleasure. The mother realizes that although her child may have avoided the effort of having to toil for a living, or investing in emotional relationships, the child has also missed out on the true purpose of life.[95]

Ironically, when we try to eliminate stress from our lives, we actually *increase* it by cutting ourselves off from real life.[96] Imagine you are playing a competitive, but

---

logical pairing. He means to tell us, perhaps, that as one acquires more knowledge, he feels more acutely the pain of futility. One, therefore, is driven to move away from mere indulgences, and move toward that which is more meaningful.

95. There is no word for "doubt" in *Lashon Hakodesh* (the Holy Tongue—the Hebrew language). Our Rabbis tell us that if a word does not exist in the Torah, then it does not exist in reality. Indeed, doubt is a mixture of reality and illusion, where a person cannot see his reality clearly. Additionally, there is no word for entertainment. The idea of getting genuine pleasure from something that is without meaning is not real, and therefore not possible.

96. Just as a task will needlessly complicate itself, our mind, without an active, productive focus, will mushroom a minor concern or stress until it consumes all our time and attention.

exciting, sport. At a certain point in the game, you become injured, but because you are so focused on the sport, you do not feel the pain. Of course, after the game, or the following day, you will likely feel your injury, but as long as you are in the game, you are not distracted by pain. Now let us imagine a different scenario. Instead of being actively involved in the sport, you are a spectator, and you are sitting in the bleachers watching the game. If you get a splinter, or if the weather changes suddenly, you will instantly notice the pain or change in temperature.[97]

It gets worse. A further consequence of escapism is an inability to let go of worrisome and pervasive thoughts.[98] We literally bring our distress to life by

69

97. Those who are emotionally healthy suffer from less physical pain. Endorphins are endogenous morphines produced by the body to regulate pain by decreasing the amount of pain transmitter taken up by neurons in the brain. More endorphins mean fewer pain impulses. (Healy, Eamonn, Stewards University, Endorphins.) Anxiety, stress, and social fear are linked with endorphin discharge. A person generally exhibits decreased endorphin levels after being exposed to emotional stresses. (Laughlin, M. & Johnson, R. "Premenstrual syndrome," 101 *American Family Physician*, 29 (3): 265–269.)

98. Biologically speaking, this process depletes crucial neurotransmitters such as serotonin, forcing one to medicate in order to compensate for one's manner of thinking. Serotonin is a neurotransmitter found in the brain. It is involved in motor functioning, appetite and sleep control, and hormone regulation. Serotonin levels are affected by stress. Studies have shown that stress causes an excessive uptake of serotonin. In

giving a negative thought or impulse more attention than it deserves.[99] We give it the energy to sustain itself.[100] To a large extent, when we redirect our focus, it loses its pull. When our perspective is narrow, we cannot do this, and we lose control of our thoughts, until they become all-consuming.[101]

Pain is not the Enemy

Concerning the benefits of physical pain, how dangerous would life be if we did not have pain receptors? If we

conditions of continued exposure to stress, this high turnover rate causes depletion of serotonin in the brain that may ultimately result in depression. (Anisman, H. and R. Zacharko. "Depression: The predisposing influence of stress." *The Behavioral and Brain Sciences.* 5: 89–137.)

99. It's a lot like quicksand. While falling into it isn't quite as dire as one might believe, the victim's agitated movements do make things worse, causing the person to sink more deeply. Quicksand is denser than the human body. Therefore, if a victim remains calm, he can simply float to safety.

100. A person who is ruled by passion (and chaotic thoughts) will never be able to satisfy his endless desires. About this we learn that, "He who satisfies it is hungry; he who starves it is satisfied" (*Sanhedrin* 107).

101. A study pitted Prozac against a three-month course of psychotherapy to see which would be more effective at treating severe obsessive compulsive disorders. Those in therapy learned to turn their attention away from their compulsive feelings as soon as they began to surface. The findings showed that psychotherapy and medication proved almost equally effective, helping about two-thirds of the patients to control

accidentally leaned against a hot stove and did not feel the heat, our flesh would burn. We would limp around with broken bones and cause ourselves more damage. Could we say that a person is better off not feeling the pain?

Pain is not an obstacle to growth.[102] It is a necessary catalyst for growth to occur, or we would never budge.[103]

---

their impulses. (Baxter, L.R., et al.: Caudate glucose metabolic rate changes with both drug and behavioral therapy for obsessive-compulsive disorder. *Archives of General Psychiatry* 49, pp. 681–689, 1992.)

102. King Solomon writes: "To everything there is a season, and a time to every purpose under the heaven: a time to be born, and a time to die; a time to plant, and a time to pluck up that which is planted; a time to kill, and a time to heal; a time to break down, and a time to build up; a time to weep, and a time to laugh; a time to mourn, and a time to dance; a time to cast away stones, and a time to gather stones together; a time to embrace, and a time to refrain from embracing; a time to seek, and a time to lose; a time to keep, and a time to cast away; a time to rend, and a time to sew; a time to keep silent, and a time to speak; a time to love, and a time to hate; a time of war, and a time of peace" (Ecclesiastes 3:1–9). Jewish tradition recognizes the process of mourning, moving from total absorption in grief, to complete re-engagement in everyday life. At each stage, the time between death and burial (*aninut*), the seven days following burial (*shivah*), the first 30 days after burial (*shloshim*), the first year, and then beyond. A transformation takes root, and it moves us through the experience. Of course we feel pain—it is a part of the process—but suffering comes as a result of getting stuck along the way.

103. God does not test us in the traditional sense, as God knows what we will do. We may realize the benefits of running two miles each day, but at the end of the year, are we in better shape simply because we have this knowledge, or do we actually need to move in the physical world in

Pain brings the possibility of manifesting suppression and distraction, anger and arrogance, or gratitude and humility.[104] The opportunity allows us to activate free will and move closer to pleasure or still further away. Suffering is the emotional consequence of the wrong choice.[105]

If we look around, we will notice that there are certain people in the world who, no matter how fortunate their circumstances, they are not happy, while there are those who endure unimaginably painful situations, yet

order to see results? So, too, with our soul: growth comes through actualizing our potential, not by simply recognizing it.

104. "Do not judge your fellow until you are in his place" (Ethics of the Fathers 2:5). We cannot ever stand in anyone's place, because we do not know his potential, or the nature of his struggles; we must never assume, then, that an individual is not trying hard enough, to choose responsibly.

105. The Chofetz Chaim stated that everyone must have concerns in his life. The choice of whether they are spiritual or mundane, however, is entirely up to us. By taking actions that reduce one's ego, we can feel the pain of those around us. The self-absorbed person who lacks compassion is barred from feeling the pain of others, and thus becomes immersed in his own suffering, which, unless it creates positive movement, is an unnecessary product of his own doing.

It is up to each person to choose whether he feels another's pain or his own. "If one takes upon himself the yoke of Torah, then the yoke of the government and the yoke of the worldly responsibilities are removed from him. But if someone throws off the yoke of Torah from himself, the yoke of government and the yoke of worldly responsibilities are placed upon him" (Ethics of the Fathers 3:6).

are content and calm.[106] Within each situation we create our own reality, and control how we experience the entirety of our lives.[107]

106. The Romans arrested Rabbi Akiva and executed him by brutally tearing the skin off his body with hot iron forks. As he was being tortured, Rabbi Akiva joyously recited the Shema blessing—"Hear O Israel, the Lord our God, the Lord is One." He smiled to his students in the moment just prior to his death saying that he was overjoyed to have finally discovered how to serve God with all of his being. Pain itself is a reality, while suffering is generated by illusion, and, with proper perspective, passes through us harmlessly, neither deflected by the ego nor absorbed by the soul. While eliminating *all* suffering from our lives is a theoretical and not practical possibility, we can radically alter our overall attitude and disposition.

107. Neuropsychologists have discovered that when we focus on pain, the changes in the cerebral cortex make us more sensitive to suffering. Neurologically speaking, suffering becomes programmed, and those who are preoccupied with their suffering intensify their perception of it. (Flor, H. *Spouses and Chronic Pain*. Lecture, Annual Meeting of the Society of Neuroscience, Orlando, November 3, 2002.)

CHAPTER 8

THE INFLUENCE OF SELF-ESTEEM

"According to the effort is the reward."
—ETHICS OF THE FATHERS 5:269

To the degree we lack self-esteem our psyche is plagued by desires, fleeting impulses, and urges that twist and pull at our thoughts. When we are alone, in order to quiet the unconscious voice that whispers, "I don't like me," we do whatever we can to feel good and numb the pain.[108] We spiral downward, because a person who has a poor self-image often seeks the temporary, hollow refuge of immediate gratification, and gives in to his impulses instead of rising above them.[109]

---

108. Maimonides (*Hilchot Issurei Bi'ah* 22:21) writes that one should open oneself to Torah and widen one's mind with wisdom as a means of controlling impulses, for the desire and the lust for immorality only reside in a heart that is devoid of wisdom.

109. Our primary reason for indulging in earthly pleasures is to suppress

When the ego reigns, our emotions cloud our thoughts, and our choices are unproductive and sometimes harmful.[110] When we do not like who we are—which again, is true for all human beings, to varying degrees—we punish ourselves with activities that are disguised as pleasurable: excessive eating, alcohol or drug abuse, and endless, meaningless distractions. We desperately want to *love* ourselves, but instead we *lose* ourselves. Unable to invest in our own wellbeing, we substitute illusions for love. These ethereal pleasures mask our self-contempt, and because the comfort sought is rewarded instead by greater pain, we descend further into despair.[111]

Have you ever chatted pleasantly with someone whom you did not like very much? How about spending

and deflect our deficiencies, which reflect, at the core, a spiritual hunger (*Michtav M'Eliyahu*, vol. 1, p. 100).

110. Moses tells the Jewish people, "And you should know that not because of your righteousness does the Lord your God give you this good land to possess it, for you are a stiff-necked people" (Deuteronomy 9:6). Rabbi Ovadia Sforno, a great Italian sixteenth-century commentator, explains that it is impossible to be righteous if one is stiff-necked and always follows one's emotions instead of listening to reason and acting in accordance with one's intellect.

111. The egocentric person demands to know, "Why is this is happening to me?", until the pain becomes too intense for his ego to deflect. At that point he begins to ask, "Why" from a place of humility and utter helplessness. One reason why an addict may finally get better after hitting rock bottom is because his ego is so dented that he can see what has become of his life with an acuity and clarity that had been long gone.

an hour or an entire day with someone who got on your nerves? It's almost painful. What if you lived with that person . . . and that person was you?

Everything in life is draining for the person who does not like who he has become. It's like working for a boss you despise. Even the most minor task triggers annoyance. Would you work hard for or invest in, let alone love and respect, an ungrateful and out-of-control person?

A Mind in Prison

The egocentric person indulges his impulses and seeks the approval of others. In other words, his life is not his own; this dependence creates a sense of helplessness. This is the source of superstition: it sets in when we lose the capacity to distinguish between what we can and cannot control in life. The relationship between cause and effect is blurred. This can make us virtual slaves to rituals and compulsive behaviors. We need to feel some sense of control, so we draw our own correlation between an event and a behavior. If we knock three times, then the meeting will go well, and so on. These types of behavior give us a feeling of empowerment.

When we do not believe that we can impact our own lives, we lose the will to do anything that takes effort—especially that which does not have a direct and guaranteed pay-off.

To be emotionally healthy, we need to believe that if we take action X, it can influence result Y. *Learned helplessness*, a term coined by psychologist Martin Seligman, occurs when a person feels that since he is not in control, he might as well give up. Seligman maintains that people have a perception of helplessness when they believe that their actions will not be able to influence their outcomes.[112]

As an analogy, full-grown circus elephants are kept tethered with small ropes looped around one leg. They don't try to break free because they have been tethered in this way since they were young and weak. After trying repeatedly to break free without success, they give up. As adult elephants, they could easily tear the whole circus tent down and move about at will, but they have learned to be helpless, so they don't even try.[113]

112. The healthiest mentality is when we put forth our full effort, while recognizing that we do not cause the outcome. This is quite different from one who does not feel that his actions will impact, in any way, his happiness and wellbeing.

113. Multiple experiments show that individuals who are exposed to unpleasant conditions which they cannot control will afterwards become withdrawn. In one such experiment, subjects were exposed to extremely high levels of noise. By pushing a button one group could stop the noise while the other could not stop the noise. A short while later when both groups were brought together, individuals from the group who could do nothing about the noise—and were helpless—when asked to participate in a sport or game, showed little interest or motivation to win (Hiroto, D.: Locus of control and learned helplessness, In: *Journal of Experimental Psychology*, 20, 1974).

Our Personality is Formed

Since self-esteem and the ego are mutually exclusive, there is no such thing as a person with high self-esteem *and* an inflated ego. When our self-esteem begins to erode, our perspective shrinks, and more of our personality comes through, filtered by our own insecurities. As a result, two distinct mentalities are produced: one can have low self-esteem *and* a dented (though not diminished) ego—this is the doormat mentality. And one can have low self-esteem and an inflated ego—this is the arrogant person. Two people, therefore, with low self-esteem, can manifest one of two different attitudes toward the same situation. Let us gain a deeper clarity of these types.

> ▶ **Low self-esteem, dented ego:** This person is quick to apologize, even when something is not his fault. He does things for others he does not really want to do, for fear of not being liked. He rarely stands up for himself, as he does not feel that his needs are important enough, and certainly not more important than others. He is a quintessential people pleaser. While he feels unworthy of good fortune and happiness, he is still egocentric as the world revolves around his pain. The difference is that he is unable to voice his dissatisfaction and assert himself, so he may seek passive-aggressive ways to "even the score."

► **Low self-esteem, inflated ego:** This person needs to be the center of attention, is often loud, easily frustrated, and a big complainer. He is often a fierce competitor whose self-worth hangs in the balance of every competition. When he gives his opinion, he is often offended when his ideas are rejected. He insists people understand his point of view, and if a person were to argue with him, he would blame the other person for being too stubborn to take his good advice. This person can often be seen hitting, banging, and forcing inanimate objects to do his will. Just as he tries to do with people, he insists on imposing his will onto things and demanding they take heed.

These mentalities are not usually fixed. A person with low self-esteem often fluctuates between personas of inferiority (the doormat mentality) and superiority (producing arrogance), depending on the dominant personality mode at any given time. When a person is feeling inferior, he directs the negativity inward, manifesting hurt and sadness, and when a person is feeling superior, he directs the negativity outward, resulting in anger.

All of us, from time to time, vacillate between mindsets. As the Chassidic saying goes, "A person should carry two pieces of paper in his pocket. One that says, 'I am nothing but dust,' and the other that says 'The world was created only for my sake.'" The secret, it notes, is knowing which piece of paper to pull out when.

This seemingly simple Chassidic quote unleashes a wealth of wisdom regarding human nature. To the degree that we lack self-esteem, we react to the situation with the wrong mentality or "piece of paper." In a situation where our ego is threatened, if we have high self-esteem, we are able to perceive that we are "nothing but dust." But when we suffer from low self-esteem, we erroneously believe that the world was created only for us, and we feel slighted and hurt by anyone who challenges us along the way.

CHAPTER 9

MIND OVER MATTERS

"Blessed is the man who trusts in God, who makes God his refuge."
—Jeremiah 17:79

While a person with perspective will see the irrelevance in a circumstance that might easily consume his egocentric counterpart, the question we are faced with is, "How do we manage what is relevant?" To answer this, we will turn our discussion to the subject of trust, and explore how self-esteem gives us access to a whole new level of calm.

Difficult times and tragic events challenge our coping skills.[114] As humans, our perspective is finite, making it difficult for us to see the bigger picture. Still, we can

---

114. *Sichot Mussar* 53 discusses that we are most vulnerable while experiencing a downturn. The key is to keep our head above water as well as possible until the situation stabilizes, lest we continue on a downward spiral. See also *Orchot Tzadikim 2* (*Sha'ar Anavah*).

gain peace of mind and derive comfort during difficult times when we develop the capacity to trust, which then serves as a surrogate to our sight.[115] In that way, we become immune to distress, because we do not have to see something with our two eyes in order to accept that the outcome is for our ultimate benefit.

We cannot trust in God, however, beyond the scope of our behavior. When we make a poor choice, we are not acknowledging God; and to the degree that He is not in our lives, we cannot have a relationship with Him, let alone trust in Him.[116] The chasm widens afterward when we justify our actions, which continues to engage the ego, and pushes God still further away.

BEYOND FAITH

The ability to exercise self-control eliminates anxiety as it moves us beyond *emunah* (faith) and into *bitachon*

---

115. "Cast your burden upon the Lord and He will sustain you" (Psalms 55:23). "Blessed is the man who made God his trust, and did not turn to the arrogant or those who stray after falsehood" (ibid. 40:5).

116. Trust, which is essential to every relationship, exists when we do what is asked of us, regardless of whether or not it makes sense intellectually. Avraham Avinu (Abraham) was told by God to sacrifice his only son. This command made no sense, as God had promised him that his offspring would multiply like the stars in the sky. Yet, Abraham did as God commanded, because he trusted Him.

(trust). The difference is profound. We can have *faith* that things will work out, but may still be plagued by worry and fleeting moments of doubt. When we have *trust*, however, negative thoughts do not fill our mind. We do not dwell on, or worry about, the outcome. Trust is an intellectual process which is the natural outgrowth of our positive choices, and exists independent of our mood or emotional state.[117]

We intuit that with each action, there is a natural consequence. When we engage in conduct that we know to be wrong, no matter how masterfully we justify it, the unconscious voice of our soul cries out. While it is often muffled by the ego, we wait unconsciously for the universe to drop the other proverbial shoe. By doing what is right, we are no longer consumed with guilt and torn by impulse.[118]

Imagine the following scenario: a thief walks into a grocery store, steals a loaf of bread, and then flees, probably looking over his shoulder nervously for the negative consequences of his actions. For a while after the adventure, he will be obsessed with what may happen. (Just as

---

117. A loss of control or self-respect—either real or imagined—always precedes a bad mood, and causes our faith to waiver.
118. "Trust in God brings happiness and joy. He who trusts in God has peace of mind and tranquility of the soul" (*Chovot Halevavot*). "One who trusts in God does not grieve if denied a request or if deprived of something he loves" (ibid.).

a person braces himself physically in anticipation of being hit, so, too, do we brace ourselves emotionally when we feel vulnerable.) If the thief had not stolen the bread, such anxiety would not exist.

Those who are in control of themselves recognize that they are not in control of the world, and are therefore free of worry.[119] Moreover, exercising self-control offers solace, since we are cognizant of the fact that we have done as much as we can, and trust that God will take care of the rest. Those who lack self-control mistakenly believe that they are in control of their circumstances, and therefore easily become neurotic, angry, and frustrated.

According to research, individuals with high life change scores (indicating that a person is experiencing multiple changes in his life at one time) are more likely to fall ill, but most surprisingly, studies reveal that the illness correlates with *any type of change*.[120] Whether the event is positive or negative bears no consequence on the stress experienced; the circumstances are largely irrelevant, but

---

119. Emotional instability has its roots in feelings of inadequacy (low self-esteem) and helplessness (lack of control). Even with specific illnesses, from obsessive-compulsive disorder to phobias, the emotional stress that contributes to the underlying illness is the same: a loss of control lies at the center of these emotional distortions. Chemical imbalance or genetic predisposition will increase the susceptibility, but it is the stress of a situation that creates the spark.

120. Holmes, T. & Rahe, R. (1967): "Social readjustment rating scale," *Journal of Psychosomatic Research*, vol. 11, p. 214.

the ability to feel in control is imperative. This is exactly why we may find ourselves engaging in self-destructive behavior even when things in our life are going well; it is not about the circumstances, it's about whether or not we feel the need to control the situation.[121]

In direct proportion to the quality of our choices is our ability to free ourselves from worry and to trust in the outcome. The path to peace of mind is paved not by circumstance, but by choice.

---

121. Overwhelming evidence supports this idea across a range of environments. Research shows that residents of an old age home who were given more autonomy—such as the ability to make strictly minor decisions, along the line of being able to choose meal options from a menu, instead of being served the "day's fare," and having the ability to choose from several destinations for short outings—were not as prone to sickness, and the annual death rate was *cut in half.* (Rodin, J.: "Aging and Health. Effects of the sense of control." *Behavioral Brain Res.* 1994).

CHAPTER **10**

TURNING GUILT INTO ACTION

*"Happy is one who is pardoned of trans-
gression and forgiven of sin."*

—PSALMS 32:1

Have you ever noticed that when you are angry with
yourself, you are more prone to bang into things or
knock them over? [122] Such behavior is an unconscious

---

122. Anger significantly increases a person's chances of injury, according to a study of more than 2,500 patients who had been seriously
injured and sought care in the emergency room. Researchers led by
Dr. Daniel Vinson found that 31.7% reported some degree of irritabil-
ity just before the injury, 18.1% reported feeling angry, and 13.2%
reported feeling hostile. The relationship between anger and injury was
also found to be stronger in men than in women. *Annals of Family
Medicine* 4:63–68 (2006).

Rashi, commenting on the Midrash, says that whenever Moses
became angry with the people, he erred in some way (Numbers 31:21).
He rebuked them for boldly demanding water, and he then produced
water by hitting the rock rather than speaking to it (ibid. 20:1–13). He

attempt to get back at ourselves because we made a decision that we knew was not right, even though we could not help ourselves at the time. Guilt is a negative force that weighs us down, causing us to engage in unconsciously-motivated self-destructive behavior.[123]

We must be able to forgive our own mistakes. Taking responsibility is not about being perfect, but about what we do when we discover that we have faltered, and how we move forward to make right when we have done wrong. Guilt is useless unless it creates the impetus for action, in which case what we really have is regret.

We cannot "talk away" or rationalize our guilt. The way to fully alleviate this pain is prescribed by the Torah.[124] The following four-step process can morph our negative feelings into positive emotions, turn guilt into regret,

rebuked Israel for keeping alive the wicked daughters of Midyan after their successful battle, and he then neglected to teach a relevant law (ibid. 31:1–24). The *Vitry Machzor* elaborates on the theme that people do not think straight when they are angry.

123. "A person who repents should not imagine that he is distant from being righteous on account of his past. It is not so. Rather, he is beloved and cherished before the Creator as if he has never sinned" (Rambam, *Teshuva* 7:4).

124. How does a person still feel guilty, even when God forgives him? Does he hold himself to a higher standard than God? No. He is not being noble, he is being selfish. He wraps himself in guilt, to avoid facing himself, his actions, and his life. It is the height of irresponsibility, beyond whatever action led to his feelings of guilt.

and turn regret into action. So crucial to our emotional wellbeing is this process that the Talmud tells us that before God created the world, He created the power of *teshuva* (repentance).[125]

1. Feel remorseful. Sincere regret for our wrong actions is the first step towards releasing our guilt. We must be genuinely ashamed over our actions, or we cannot truly be sorry for them.

2. Stop the behavior. If it was a one-time action, then there is nothing more to stop. However, if we are still engaging in the behavior that we feel bad about, then we must stop it. If we cannot stop ourselves immediately, then we must create a plan to stop this behavior over a period of time, and we must then stick to the plan. We need to create deterrents for ourselves in order to avoid repeating the same transgression. In this way, we make a statement to ourselves and others that we have changed and that we are taking action to ensure that our improved selves thrive.

3 Confess before God. By confessing before God, we offer aloud the commitments and sentiments that reside in our heart. We should say, "I have sinned with (this behavior), I deeply regret my actions, and I declare

---

125. "Great is *Teshuva*, that it preceded the creation of the world" (*Midrash Tehillim* 90:12).

before God, Who knows my innermost thoughts, that I will never do this sin again."

For sins committed against other people, we must first ask forgiveness from that person before God will accept the *teshuva*. If we have wronged a person, we must seek to make amends. We are not responsible for the other person's response, but we do have to ask. If this person does not accept our apology—after three separate attempts—then perhaps this person is not meant to be in our life, and that is for our benefit, and depending upon his motive, it is for his benefit as well.*

4 Resolve not to do it again. Acceptance for the future requires us to resolve, in our hearts, never to commit the sin again.

*THE POWER OF AN APOLOGY

Letting go is freedom. This explains the feeling of relief that floods us after we apologize to someone. It also explains why we feel lighter. Real power comes from apologizing for the sake of doing the right thing, and not because the situation calls for such a response. Of course, it is very empowering to apologize when we know we are in the wrong—but this behavior, while it does dilute the ego, is still a response to circumstance, and therefore dependency is naturally inherent. When we apologize to someone, even if that person doesn't

necessarily deserve an apology, we exercise free will at its
highest level.[126]

A Fresh Start

In a later chapter we will further discuss the remarkable
power of forgiveness. Our need to forgive others though,
extends beyond the stated benefits, because it is the
preparatory stage to *teshuva*. If we forgive others, God
tells us that He will forgive our transgressions.[127] Indeed,
teshuva wipes the spiritual slate clean.[128]

126. Respect lies at the crux of establishing peace in any situation. This
means that we should not argue and scream our point, or show up at
our friend's office demanding that he listen to our side of the story.
Approaching the situation with respect is vital to our success. It is also
important to take full and complete responsibility for our actions. Do
not shift blame or assign excuses—this will only exacerbate the situation. Finally, we need to apologize for our behavior. Sometimes we
forget to actually say the words, "I'm sorry."

127. "Whose sins does He forgive? The sins of one who overlooks an
injustice committed against him" (Rosh Hashanah 17a).

128. *Teshuva* allows us to erase deeds for which we feel shame; it does
not affect deeds for which we feel embarrassment. What's the difference?
Embarrassment exists in public; it is the result of the ego protecting the
image. Shame, the voice of our soul, exists in private; it involves feeling
bad about our actions—regardless of whether anyone else knows of
them—simply because we know that the actions are inherently wrong.
Those who do what they know is not right, in order to spare themselves
embarrassment now, will undoubtedly feel the pain of shame later.

How does this work? How is it possible to erase our past mistakes, as if they never happened? [129] The ability to do so defies the laws of human logic, yet is as real as gravity. Moving backwards in time is unnatural. For that matter, emotional growth itself is unnatural. When we release our egos and take responsibility, we free ourselves from the confines of time. Admitting that we did something wrong goes against our nature, but when we do so, God rises above nature for us, and He undoes the damage that has been done. [130]

94

---

129. When we perform *teshuva* properly, the sin becomes a *mitzvah* (a good deed) and a negative act is transformed into a positive one. There is a physical correlation to this unnatural reversal. When we break a bone in our body, the set bone, once properly healed, is usually thicker and even stronger than the uninjured bone surrounding the break. If we break the same bone again, it's unlikely to be at the same spot.

130. "By loving-kindness and truth shall sin be atoned" (Proverbs 15:6).

SECTION

IV

RESHAPING
OUR
RELATIONSHIPS

CHAPTER **11**

HOW TO LOVE AND BE LOVED

"You shall love your neighbor as yourself."
—LEVITICUS 19:18

If we think of the people we know who are emotionally
healthy, they generally have positive relationships.
Conversely, those who don't seem to get along with anyone are often emotionally unstable. Our self-esteem has
a direct impact on the quality of our relationships.

To the degree that we lack self-esteem, we cannot
love ourselves fully. To fill this emotional void, we turn
to the world for approval. This behavior illuminates the
source of all negative emotions and interpersonal conflicts. The acceptance and recognition that we crave
comes in the form of respect. We erroneously believe
that if only others would respect us, we would be able to
respect ourselves by converting the adoration and praise

of others into self-love. Our self-worth is therefore dependent on others' opinions.

When we depend on others for validation, we become tense and vulnerable, as we over-analyze every fleeting glance and passing comment. It does not matter how much respect and adoration we receive; we are like a cup without a bottom: the moment we stop receiving this undivided attention, we are as empty and as thirsty as we were before. Yes, there are moments of fleeting satisfaction, but ultimately we remain empty inside.

No-Win or Win-Win

A sense of self-esteem endows us with the ability to give. To the degree that we do not like ourselves, we cannot receive, we can only take. The more self-esteem we have, the more we are whole, as receiving is a natural consequence of giving. This cycle of giving and receiving creates the perfect union. When we take, however, we do so in an attempt to fill a void—leaving us still empty, and forced, once again, to take in a vain attempt to feel complete. Such behavior only reinforces our dependency, and continues to exhaust us emotionally, spiritually, and physically.[131] Man is the sum total of what he gives; and he loses a piece of himself every time he takes.

---

131. Research into heart disease by psychologist Larry Scherwitz found

Along these lines, those who believe that marriage is only a partnership are mistaken. Emotionally speaking, a healthy union has nothing to do with two halves coming into a relationship to make each other whole. Two people who seek to become whole by taking from the other cannot become one.

Without enough self-esteem, every relationship is rigged for a no-win scenario. For example, someone asks us for a favor, but we do not want to do it, for good reason. Giving out of fear or guilt does nothing to enhance self-esteem. To the contrary, it diminishes it. Such a situation is not really giving; it is the other person taking. If we acquiesce, then we are angry at ourselves or the other person, and if we do not do it, we feel guilty. Whatever we do leads to further justification; we cannot win. The ego swells in both scenarios and neither situation boosts self-esteem.

Through this paradigm we learn how to tell if someone has high or low self-esteem. It is reflected in how he

---

incontrovertible evidence that self-absorbed people had more severe coronary disease than their less egocentric counterparts. In a study of 150 patients who were hospitalized for heart disease, Dr. Scherwitz monitored how often these patients use the words "I," "me," "my," "mine," or "myself" during a structured interview. His conclusions show that the patients with more severe disease gave longer answers and had more self-references (Redford Williams, M.D., and Virginia Williams, Ph.D. *Anger Kills*. Harper Perennial, Harper Collins. 1994).

treats himself and others.[132] A person who lacks self-esteem may indulge in things to satisfy only his own desires, and he will not treat others particularly well (a product of an arrogant mentality). Alternatively, this person may cater to others because he so craves their approval and respect, but he does not take care of his own needs (a product of the doormat mentality). Only someone who has higher self-esteem is able to give—love, respect, time, and attention—to both himself and to others.

GIVING VS. TAKING

When a person gives, he loves the object of his giving more—and so love is planted and grows.[133] A child

---

132. When we are treated poorly by someone without apparent justification, it is almost always because that person does not feel good about himself. If, however, we provide the person with his emotional needs, then the response will usually be completely different. Research examined sixty-nine studies about influencing impressions and getting a person to like us. Of all tactics, the most successful was simply making the other person feel good about himself, whether through sincere flattery, compliments, or praise. In fact, doing favors was the least effective. The bottom line is that people crave to feel good about themselves and most people are forced to rely on others to nourish them. Gordon, R.A. (1996). "Impact of ingratiation on judgments and evaluations: A meta-analytical investigation." *Journal of Personality and Social Psychology*, 71, 51–70.

133. There is no escaping that fact that a parent gives because the child is, in some way, an extension of him. This is ego. Why will a parent

receives and a parent gives; who loves who more? The child cannot wait to get out of the house, while the parent is forever concerned with the child's wellbeing.

Every positive emotion stems from giving and flows outward from us to others, whereas every negative emotion revolves around taking.[134] Indeed, the root of the Hebrew word, *ahavah*, love, is *hav*, to give.

Lust is the opposite of love. When we lust after someone or something, our interest is purely selfish in our desire to feel complete.[135] When we love, however, our focus is on how we can express our love, and give to the other person. It makes us feel good to give, and we do so happily.[136] When someone we love is in pain, we feel pain. When someone after whom we lust is in pain, however, we think only about how this person's

sacrifice so much for his child, but not for the kid down the block? He loves his child, yes, but to some extent the love derives from the knowledge that it is his child.

134. *Michtav Me'eliyahu* Vol. 1 (*Kuntres Hachesed*).

135. With the understanding that the ego separates man from God, it is clear that, "One who becomes separated from God seeks lust" (Proverbs 18:1).

136. Ramban (on Leviticus 19:18) asks how one can fulfill the commandment to, "Love your neighbor as much as yourself," if it's impossible to love a friend as much as oneself. He explains that the Torah commands us to wish that our friend shares the same good fortune that befalls us (i.e., wealth, health, etc.), and be happy when he receives it, even when his success is greater than ours. This commandment, which is the foundation of helping others, is rooted in healthy self-esteem.

situation will affect us, in terms of our own inconvenience or discomfort.

Love is limitless. A parent does not love her second child less because she already has one child.[137] She loves each child, gives to each child, and does not run out of love. Compare this to someone who acquires a work of art that he "loves." Over time, his fascination with the piece wanes, and when he acquires a new work, all of his attention, affection, and joy is redirected from the old art to the new art because, in truth, he does not love his art. He loves himself, and his art makes him happy. He is not giving to his art; his art gives to him, and so he takes.[138]

137. It is common for a parent to favor one child over another. It occurs almost always for one of two reasons. Either the child was ill or for some reason especially needy, in which case the parent gave more; this in turn increases our love, as the more you give the more you love. Or the child is brighter, more attractive, more charismatic than the others, in which case again, our ego makes us more proud, more connected to this child, because we feel that the child's attributes reflect well upon ourselves.
138. Our feelings of self-worth betray us when we consider whether God really cares about little old me, with all the billions of people in the world. There are no limitations to God's love. He created the world expressly for us as if we were His only child. Just as a loving parent is concerned and consumed by each and every aspect of the child's wellbeing, so, too, is God's interest in our lives.

CHAPTER 12

DIFFICULT PEOPLE: THE
SOLUTION, NOT THE PROBLEM

"Seek peace and pursue it."
—Psalms 34:15

The below image demonstrates negative space. Focus on the white image and we see a vase; focus on the black space and we see two profiles facing each other. Each space, positive and negative, defines the other. The vase cannot maintain the integrity of its shape unless the white space does the same.

No matter how much we work on ourselves, we will never be successful at transforming any aspect of our character, if our new self cannot exist in our world. Reshaping ourselves into the desired vessel can only be accomplished by redefining current relationships, and better understanding the role that difficult people play in our lives.

Flight attendants begin each trip by informing passengers that in the event of the oxygen masks dropping down during the flight, those traveling with children should secure their own masks first, and then secure the masks on their children. We are no good to anyone if we are no good to ourselves. Whenever we redraw lines in relationships, one person gets less territory; but without boundaries, there is no definition of self. While some relationships benefit from having no boundaries, allowing those who are toxic make the rules and shape us is not healthy. It certain instances, then, we are obligated to say, "Enough is enough."[139]

We are mistaken to believe that the larger solution is cutting out of our lives those people who are difficult; rarely is this required. It is only when we respond to another's' cruelty with like, that we move to a mode of dependence, and so pain. There is no way to get around this. Guilt will seep in, our ego engages to fortify our actions and our beliefs, and all the while, our self-esteem and emotional wellbeing slowly melt.

Sometimes, the closer we are to someone, the worse we treat them. Too often, a person shows more gratitude

139. Unless extraordinary circumstances exist, it is fundamental to our emotional and spiritual wellbeing to maintain the healthiest possible relationships with our immediate family—parents, siblings, spouse, and children. While all relationships are important, familial relationships are crucial; strive to make them as positive and healthy as possible.

to the toll collector than to his own spouse; indeed, sometimes we deliver kindness to a stranger but ignore the needs of our own family.

One reason we do not give is because we do not get. A person holds back from another because he does not feel that his own emotional needs are being met. On the other side of the coin, strangers are quick to offer their appreciation and to give us the respect we crave when we come to their aid. Will a family member even acknowledge our efforts? It does not matter. Our actions must be independent of the response or of our own feelings of whether or not the other party in the relationship deserves our kindness and love.

The temptation to do otherwise is strong, particularly if we suffer from low self-esteem. By definition, low self-esteem means that a person does not feel in control—remember, self-respect comes from self-control. So the less control we exert over ourselves, the more we attempt to control or manipulate the world and the people in it.[140]

---

140. Correspondingly, we can ask any parent about child-rearing's two most difficult phases. The answer is invariably the "terrible twos" and the teenage years. This pattern is easily understood in terms of control and respect. A two-year-old is gaining a sense of independence and freedom and wants to exercise this instinct. The teenager also wants to express his individuality. In both scenarios, the parents seek to control, and conflict ensues. Both parties lack the control they want and neither feels respected.

Now we understand why it is that we hurt—either overtly or passive aggressively—the ones closest to us. The closer we are to someone, the more power we have over them, and the more we can attack their weaknesses with pinpoint accuracy.[141] When we lack self-control, hurting those who love us gives us the most traction to cause something to happen. It is the last vestige of power for the person who has so little of it.[142]

We know from our own lives that we do not feel complete when we are feuding or estranged from a member of our immediate family.[143] But as we noted, God does not leave our wellbeing at the doorstep of other people, let alone those who are not well. If we do everything that we can, when we can, for as long as we can, to have the healthiest relationship possible, and we still

---

141. The person who suffers from very low self-esteem is likely to have grown up in a home that was chaotic and unpredictable. He attempts to control others as a way to predict their behavior.

142. When a person has very low self-esteem, it does not matter how accomplished he appears; such a person is dependent upon everyone and everything to feed his ego. In *Megillat Esther*, we are introduced to the wicked Haman. His behavior exemplifies the egocentric mindset. Haman has money, power, and prestige, yet becomes enraged when a single person, Mordechai, does not show him respect.

143. "Do things for the sake of their Creator and speak about them for their own sake" (*Nedarim* 62a). We should seek to make peace not because we are right, but because it is inherently right to do so, even without a so-called reason.

don't get anywhere, then we find that while we have compassion for the other, and perhaps some sadness over the loss of the relationship, we do not feel less good about ourselves.[144]

Don't Shoot the Messenger

It is our responsibility to perceive the wider reality, which is that God is speaking to us through *every* person and situation. Relationships are a very common area in which people often miss the message and focus on the messenger.[145] God does not need us to solve another

144. After decades of estrangement Jacob finally made peace with his brother Esau. Afterwards, the Torah states, "Jacob Arrived whole to the city of Shechem" (Genesis 33:18). The word for peace, *shalom*, derives from the word *shalem*, which means whole. A person who is at peace with himself and with others is complete. That said, our strife with another need not cause discord within ourselves. Our willingness to do what is necessary to bring peace, is what will give us peace (to the degree that God allows), regardless of the outcome. There is one major caveat. When we say that we need to do everything possible to make peace, we do not mean that we try our very best to make our point, and present a clear and rational argument as to why we are right. Only an attempt at peace that comes by way of complete humility, will keep our trust in God intact and our conscience absolved of guilt.
145. The Sages compare anger to idolatry. The essence of idolatry is the belief that God is not the only power influencing life. Anger assumes the same belief. "If one breaks dishes in his anger, it is as if he were involved in idol worship" (*Talmud, Shabbat* 105b).

person's problems—He is perfectly capable of solving them Himself. On a simple level, it is true that we should help others, but we must also understand the larger picture and ask ourselves the important question, "What lesson can I learn from this person?"

Difficult people are not in our lives to add to our woes, but to help us; and we need to realize this, or they will keep coming around again and again—and so may we keep coming around, again and again.[146]

When we are blatantly correct in a specific instance, we usually make an excuse as to why we have no responsibilities in that situation. The prerequisite for growing in any area is not to blame, or be enraged at the injustice of the situation, but to ask oneself practically, "What does God want from me now?"[147]

While we are in blame-mode, we are also not solution-oriented, and therefore cannot see, let alone investigate, ways to improve the situation. What would happen if you would stop looking at yourself as a victim?

---

146. *Gilgulim* (reincarnation) is the "revolving" or recycling of souls through a succession of lives, and is a central theme in Judaism. This opportunity for rectification and soul-perfection comes from our ability to make responsible choices, where previously we had missed the true meaning behind the message. The Chofetz Chaim says that most of our questions about hardships would be answered to our satisfaction if we fully understood the issue of reincarnation.

147. The expression of this theme is by Rabbi Aryeh Leib Nivin.

CHAPTER 13

BACK TO THE FUTURE

*"When asked by an offender for forgiveness,
one should forgive with a sincere mind
and a willing spirit."*
—MISHNEH TORAH, TESHUVAH 2:10

We cannot move our lives forward, unless we seal the leaks of the past, by healing our relationships with ourselves, with others, and with God. Our interest centers primarily on forgiving ourselves (which we discussed earlier) and others, because once we are free from this negativity, the ego loses its grip. As a natural consequence we move closer to God, and our relationship begins to repair itself.

In the physical world, Newton's second law—that force equals mass times acceleration (f=ma)—deals with the relationship between force and motion. Essentially, by lightening the load, an object can accelerate faster. Emotionally speaking, the application is the same.

It is a function of human design, whereby we hold on to painful experiences (physical as well as psychological) in order to learn from those experiences, and to avoid repeating them. Until we acknowledge them, they remain part of us. Think of those experiences in our lives that we refuse to release, and contrast them with those we have accepted and moved beyond.

FORGIVENESS IS GOOD FOR YOU

We should note that there are two distinct components to healing. One involves making peace with the reality, and the other involves making peace with the person. The fact that we may want nothing to do with the other person is exclusive of whether or not we (or the other person) have a desire to re-establish the relationship.

We forgive someone not because we are thinking of that person's feelings per se, but for the sake of our own emotional wellbeing. When we hold onto anger, *we suffer*, regardless of the reason or rationale.[148] Anger is the illusion of control. It is a defense mechanism against feeling vulnerable; yet, in the end, it offers no real satisfaction or

---

148. Nineteen separate studies confirm that forgiveness reduces anxiety and depression while increasing self-esteem.

psychological comfort. It intensifies the ego and makes us feel stronger. All the while, the opposite is happening, as we spiral out of control, and we become weaker with each intense, anger-driven action or reaction.

The ego tricks us into believing that by holding on to our pain, we balance out the equation, and we get back what we lost. The opposite is true. The Gemara teaches us that God creates the cure before the disease.[149] The means to heal ourselves is found in our response— in forgiveness.

If we believe that we are owed an apology, we should ask for one. However, we do not need another person to apologize to us in order for us to feel complete and at peace. We need only understand that it is a failing within the other person that does not allow him to take responsibility; it does not point out a deficiency within us.

How it all Begins

An adult's self-esteem is often damaged as a result of suffering from lack of love or experiencing intense turmoil at an early age. This is because children gain their self-esteem largely from their parents (or primary caregivers). Children do not possess the reasoning faculties to make choices as adults do, and thus they cannot gain self-

---

149. *Megillah* 13b.

respect through self-control. Our personal sense of right and wrong is not fully established until our early teens.[150] For egocentric beings (children), it is easy to ascribe a failure within ourselves as the "reason" behind a parent's behavior. A parent becomes angry with the child, and so the child naturally concludes that there is a flaw within herself. She translates her parent's anger into, "I am unworthy of his love," which soon becomes, "I am not worthy of being loved." Now, if a child can form these conclusions—as many do—with loving parents, imagine how easy it is for the child to draw the conclusion that she is unlovable or bad when she is being raised by abusive parents. The child will understandably feel, "If my parents' can do this to me, then what am I worth?"[151]

If we did not receive love from our parents as children, or felt that our lives were out of control due to trauma or domestic volatility, we may needlessly spend the rest of our lives craving love and acceptance. Everything we do is intended to bring us to that end.

---

151. This is the reasoning behind the Torah's view of a boy or girl coming of age once he reaches the age of thirteen or twelve, respectively. The Torah teaches that a child is not held completely accountable for his actions in the *Beit Din* (Rabbinical courts) until these respective ages.

152. Research by Robert Ressler, the legendary FBI behavioral scientist who coined the term serial killer, confirms that 100% of serial killers have been abused, neglected, or humiliated as children.

The love that parents give children is determined by their own limitations, not those of the children. It never occurs to us as children that maybe it has nothing to do with us.

As adults, it can still be difficult to internalize the fact that our self-worth isn't contingent upon our parents' approval of us, but we can recreate this imprint. Once we do, our lives can be forever changed, and the damage that has disfigured us for decades can be undone.

We will not find an emotionally healthy person with considerable unresolved anger towards a parent. It is highly probable that this person will have difficulty enjoying positive, let alone deep and meaningful, relationships while this anger exists. Anyone who feels anger towards a parent must make it a priority to move past the negative feelings.[152]

152. The Ten Commandments are divided into two categories: the first five contain the man-to-God mitzvot and the second five the man-to-man mitzvot. Revealingly, the fifth commandment to honor our parents is on the man-to-God side of the tablets. This is because it is not easy to love, and to feel loved, by the Creator of the universe, while holding onto negativity and pain about our parents. On many levels, the relationship between a child and a parent is symbolic of our relationship with God. Through honoring our parents, we begin to cultivate an appreciation and understanding of how much our parents love us (or perhaps try to), in spite of their finite limitations. Thus, our relationship with God is similarly enhanced.

REVISITING THE PAST

Turning our discussion back to the field of quantum mechanics, experiments reveal something most intriguing: the *quantum eraser effect*. Physicists have determined that something happening after the fact can change or "erase" the way particles have behaved at an earlier point in time. As strange as this seems, not only do we *shape* reality, but we can *recreate* what has already unfolded. This means that a shift in perspective now allows us to "undo" our past and permanently alter how we see ourselves and our world.[153]

It is difficult to grasp the concept that reality is not linear, where a shift in perspective can create retroactive change. Since human beings are locked in time and space, we cannot easily see how the future can change the past.

Imagine an elderly woman, who, after believing that she was happily married for sixty years, is told on her deathbed that her recently departed husband never loved her—he was a paid actor hired by her parents. Can we say that she was happy her entire life and that only the last thirty seconds were difficult? Did the birthday celebrations, anniversaries, walks, conversations, laughter, and memories of beautiful vacations disappear? No.

---

153. In an address to physicists, Albert Einstein pronounced: "People like us, who believe in physics, know that the distinction between past, present, and future is only a stubbornly persistent illusion."

They are there in memory, but changed. Her past is now different.

If, after hearing this revelation, someone were to ask this woman, "How was your life?" what would she answer? Would she easily answer "Wonderful?" More likely, her response would be that it was awful, sad, and heartbreaking. The characters and events are still fixed in time, but we have a glimpse of how the *now* has an impact on the *before*.

That is not to say that we should attempt to convince ourselves that our past carries no meaning. Instead, we should simply allow for the possibility that *the meaning* we have assigned to events may not be true; that how we feel about ourselves, based on how our parents (or anyone else for that matter) treated us, may be an inaccurately formed conclusion.

We continuously re-energize painful experiences by rehearsing the fictitious causal correlation between an event and our feelings. Our memory of the experience is locked in a false impression, and we file that negative memory away in our minds as fact.[154]

---

154. Breakthrough research on memory and feelings is currently being conducted. James McGaugh, a professor of neurobiology at the University of California, Irvine, discovered that our memories are highly malleable—they take time to solidify in our brains (and possibly never fully and completely solidify). Therefore, while memory is still forming, it's possible to make them stronger or weaker. It all depends on the stress

WHEN WE DON'T LET GO

We cleave to these negative thought patterns in order to manipulate reality and to cause it to unfold in accordance with our expectations. It's how we need the world to be.

So we do things against our own best interest because, unconsciously, we need to be right, in order to prove to ourselves and to others that we have been damaged. We perpetuate our own misery, ensconced in self pity.

We might assume that we need to make total and complete peace with the past before we are able to move on. This is not so. Sometimes, it is only when we move our lives forward in a meaningful direction that we are able to let go of the past and its negative associations.[155]

116

---

hormone adrenaline. When a person experiences a traumatic event, they have intense fear and helplessness which stimulates adrenaline. And then we find, days, months, or even years later, excessively strong memories. The drug Propranolol sits on that nerve cell and blocks the production of adrenaline; it is adrenaline that intensifies an experience and keeps it locked in a heighten state in memory. Therefore even after-the-fact, people who received this adrenaline-blocking drug while thinking about a past trauma, were able to form a new association to the event and in some instances, transform their feelings towards it. It becomes clear, then, that it is not the circumstance, but rather *our thoughts about the situation* that gives rise to the emotions, that determine the impact and lasting influence.

155. Multiple studies, including those conducted by The National Institute of Healthcare Research (Rockville, MD) point out that forgiveness is motivated by empathy. Once we are moving forward in our lives, the ego disengages and our ability to forgive is enhanced.

The momentum of moving allows us to shift our outlook and break free, as opposed to being stagnant and simply trying to see things differently. Taking responsibility for our lives now, wherever we are, converts the pain into fuel that ignites our emotional freedom.

SECTION

V

ACCESSING
REAL POWER

CHAPTER 14

THE FAUCET OF FORTUNE

"One who is full of haughtiness and arrogance will see his respect diminished."
—Sotah 5a

To understand man's relationship with God, we first need to recognize that God is infinite. He is everywhere and He is the source of everything. Of course, this begs the question, "If He is all that there is, then where did we come from?" Here is the short answer.

In kabbalistic terms, we understand that to create the universe, God contracted, making a part of Himself "less" in order to create a space for us to exist in this finite universe. Here is the slightly longer answer.

The act of creation is described as an act of *tzimtzum*—an act of contraction, concealment, and withdrawal. In the beginning, the "light" of God (that is, the manifest expression of His omnipresence and omnipotence) filled the entirety of existence. A finite world could not exist, for it would have been nullified within the Divine light. In order to allow for the existence of the world, God "contracted" His light, creating an empty space, and God then allowed a *kav* (single "line") of light to penetrate this void, through which flows a Divine energy that is infused into every level of reality in accordance with its capacity to receive it.[156]

As our capacity to receive expands, so is God's ability to bestow even greater blessings on us.[157]

THE POWER TO CHANGE A DECREE

Only humility expands our capacity, and to a potent extent.[158] The Sages teach us that four (according to

---

156. Our understanding of how a finite universe can exist within the Infinite is offered by one of the greatest kabbalists, The Ari, Rabbi Yitzchak Luria, who states that, "God, too, could have created a much grander and more infinite world, but He limited His omniscience as Master of the world according to our human needs" (*Da'at Tevunot* 26, 27, 52).
157. "How great is your good, stored up for those who fear You" (Psalms 31:20). The Sages interpret this to mean that God bestows on us the greatest good that we are able to receive at that time (*Midrash Tehillim* 31). Just as a physical vessel cannot hold a liquid if it is filled with leaks, our spiritual selves cannot receive from God what we cannot contain. His "ability" to bestow upon us is hinged upon our ability to receive and retain. Otherwise it does us no good, and may possibly even cause damage.
158. "God gives favor to the humble" (Proverbs 3:34).

some opinions, five) actions can actually change one's heavenly decree:[159] charity, prayer, repentance, change of our name, and change of our residence.[160] Any of these measures carry the potential to recreate our reality, saving us from many different types of suffering . . . even death.[161] What do all these actions have in common? They all promote humility.

Charity: Money gives us the illusion of power and control. It cultivates within us the idea that, with it, we are in charge of the world. Giving to others diffuses this false notion. As such, God commands us to give.

Prayer: Praying to God helps reinforce the notion of a higher power. None of us is the center of the universe, and we are not in charge.

Repentance: This is a process whereby we ask to be forgiven for our transgressions, and resolve never to commit them again. In doing so, we no longer try to justify our actions. We fully acknowledge, accept, and regret our mistakes.

Changing names: Our name is our identity. It is who we are. To change our name (as a positive improve-

123

---

159. A *gezeira milmaala* or heavenly decree denotes a quality, path, or circumstance that we are to experience. When we affect a change in character to the point that we recreate ourselves, then our decree may be changed to reflect our new selves.
160. *Rosh Hashana* 16b.
161. "Charity saves one from death" (Proverbs 10:2).

ment) is to relinquish a part of ourselves and how we see ourselves.[162]

Changing residences: We go from the known to the unknown, with hope, to a situation that shows promise of growth. We must start over in many ways and give up a lot of what is familiar and comfortable.

WE CONTROL THE VALVE

Humility is strength.[163] An arrogant person, on the other hand,[164] is an emotional junkie who depends on

162. In the Jewish faith, if a person becomes very ill, he may take on another name in an effort to change his decree.

163. The Vilna Gaon's students said that the Gemara says that a *talmid chachom* (sage) should have "one eighth of an eighth of arrogance—shmini shebi shminis" (the opposite of humility) yet the Vilna Gaon was totally humble. They asked him why. He answered cryptically, "Your own question is its own answer." When he saw that they were perplexed, he continued. "The gemara uses both masculine (shimini) and feminine (shminis) language. The Gemara should have used one or the other (masculine or feminine language) to be grammatically consistent. By changing, what lesson are the sages adding? It is reference to the eighth posuk (verse, masculine noun) of the eighth parsha (Torah portion, feminine noun), which says, 'I am too small to be worthy of all of God's kindnesses' (Genesis 32:11). When compared to God and His infinite goodness, how can any mortal person really be anything but totally humble?" Rav Leib Chasman points out (*Or Yahel*, Vol. 3, p. 93) that it's obvious that an *anav* (a humble person) isn't one who doesn't understand his strengths and capabilities; such a person isn't an *anav*, but a fool.

164. The Mishna (Ethics of the Fathers 5:19) illuminates the connection between gratitude and humility when it enumerates the contrasting

others to feed his fragile ego, and is a slave to his own impulses. As our ego seeks to distort our perception of reality in order to justify our actions, our arrogance grows, and as a result, our relationship with our Creator suffocates.

Haughtiness destroys our relationship with God, because it puts our ego in charge and pushes out our soul, leaving God with no one to talk to. The Torah states that Moses was the most humble person; he was also the greatest prophet.[165] We see that humility, reduction of ego, and prophecy go hand in hand.[166]

qualities of the students of Abraham and Bila'am. Abraham's disciples possess an *ayin tova* (they are satisfied with what they have, and readily share it with others, as seen in Proverbs 21), *ruach nemucha* (humility), and *nefesh shefela* (spirit to get along well with people). Bila'am's disciples, on the other hand, possess haughtiness, and only take from and look askance at others.

165. "No other prophet rose any more in Israel like Moses, who knew God face to face" (Deuteronomy 34:10). The Midrash says (allegorically) that when God was preparing to give the Torah, all the mountains stepped forward and stated why they thought the Torah should be given on them. In the end, God chose Mount Sinai—not because it was the tallest but because, says the Midrash, it is the most humble.

166. Since the day the Temple was destroyed, prophecy was taken from the Prophets and given to the Sages (*Bava Batra* 12a). It is no longer called prophecy; rather, it is more appropriately deemed *Ruach Hakodesh* (Divine inspiration). See also Nachmanides, *Chiddushei Ramban*, Isaiah 5:7; Chayyim Vital, *Sha'arei Kedusha* III, 6–7.

The same concept is reflected in our earthly relationships. When we love someone, we want to let that person in, emotionally and socially. To do this, we need to create a space for that person. The other, then, exists as a part of our life. And when a person creates a space for us, there is oneness, but also a sense of separateness. In a relationship, if someone is self-absorbed, then there is no room for anyone else.[167] This is why we are quite literally repelled by arrogant people, and attracted to those who are humble and put others' needs before their own.[168]

How to Love God

The wisest man who ever lived, King Solomon, ends his masterpiece, Ecclesiastes, with: "The sum of the matter,

---

167. "If the spirit of one's fellow is pleased with him, then the spirit of God is pleased with him" (Ethics of the Fathers 3:10). We find that the same ego that repulses man also repulses God; humility connects man to man, and man to God.

168. Moses was humble in that he was able to deflect all personal credit for his accomplishments. He was able to say, "Who are we?" (Exodus 16:7) with complete sincerity. Great leaders like Moses do not try to get the people to believe in them; rather they show the people how to believe in themselves and in God. By showing everyone respect and kindness, you gain the one ingredient that is essential to every great leader: charisma. This elusive trait is gained by showing people how great they are, rather than how wonderful you are.

when all has been considered, is to fear God and keep His commandments, for that is man's whole duty."[169]

At first glance, we may ask, "Why does King Solomon suggest that we should fear God rather than love Him? Isn't love a higher level of emotional attachment?" Of course we know this to be true, since the Talmud says, "Greater is the one who acts out of love, than one who acts out of fear."[170] To implement God's will out of love is greater than to do it out of fear; to repent out of love is greater than to do so out of fear. In our own relationships, when we act out of love for another, surely the relationship is healthier, stronger, and closer than when our actions are motivated by fear. So why, then, does the wise man's summation instruct us to fear God instead of telling us to strive for a greater relationship, one that is built on love?

127

The answer is that King Solomon does not tell us to love God, because love is a consequence, a result of our actions. When we fear God, we stop fearing man, since we recognize that human beings are not in control of the Universe—only God is.[171] As a result, our decisions and choices are more productive and positive, and

---

169. Ecclesiastes 12:13.
170. Talmud, *Sotah* 31a.
171. "Everything is in the hands of heaven, except for fear of heaven" (*Berachot* 32b).

consequently we gain self-esteem, which, as expected, shrinks the ego. Now we experience God in our lives. If we do not fear God, and instead direct our energy towards fearing people, or seeking comfort, vanity, and physicality, we distance ourselves from our Creator.[172] Love, then, becomes impossible because we are only taking.[173]

PLUGGED INTO REALITY

God is in our lives and in our sight, to the degree that we let Him in. This is not God playing tit-for-tat. If we do not use our free will to try to do what is right, it is as

---

172. When King Saul is pressed by Samuel about why he didn't kill Agag, the Amalekite King, as well as the animals that belonged to the Amalekites, even though he was commanded by God to destroy them, he replies, "I was afraid of the nation and I listened to their voice" (I Samuel 15:24). The question is not, "Are you afraid?", but "Who are you afraid of?" Fear God or man. You can only have one master. "Cursed is the man who trusts in man and makes flesh his strength, while his heart turns away from God" (Jeremiah 17:55).

173. Research reveals that those who place a high priority on money, success, fame, and physical appearance are *less happy* than those who strive for healthy relationships, develop their skills, and are active in social causes (Schmuck. P.; at al.: "Intrinsic and extrinsic goals: Their structure and relationship to wellbeing in German and US college students." *In Social Indicators Research* 50, 2000).

if we are saying that we do not want God in our world, and so He is not.[174]

This is precisely why we may find that our progress in life is thwarted for no apparent reason. When we cut ourselves off from the Infinite—the Source of what is good, and from the good that is bestowed on us—and find that "Pride goeth before the fall."[175] This is not simply a manner of speaking; it is how the universe works.

The second law of thermodynamics states that any closed system gradually decays toward disorder. Simply put, every entity needs an infusion of something from outside of itself, or it will eventually break down. Just as we are finite beings and need food to survive, without access to the Infinite, we cannot sustain ourselves spiritually or emotionally.[176]

129

174. Hagar became lost in the desert, ". . . then God opened her eyes. . ." (Genesis 21:19). Her focus was not on comforting her dying son, but on her own pain of having to watch him suffer. The well had existed all along but her egocentric state prevented her from seeing what was in plain sight.
175. "Pride precedes destruction, and arrogance comes before failure" (Proverbs 16:18). "God detests every arrogant person" (ibid. 16:5).
176. A perpetual motion machine which would run forever without an external source of energy is mechanically impossible, as it violates the laws of physics. Energy that is lost due to friction cannot be replaced by the machine or organism itself, and can only come from an external source.

When we are arrogant, we take God out of the equation, and say, "Look what I did!"[177] Who gave us the abilities and talents to pursue our objectives?[178] Who gave us the eyes to see and the hands to do our work? Yes, we are the ones who made the most out of our God-given gifts, which is why we should feel good about our accomplishments—but it is necessary for our emotional health, as well as our continued success, to recognize the Source of our gifts and talents.[179]

177. "One who possesses sound intellect, even if he is privileged to become a superior wise person, will understand that he has no right to feel superior to others. He is only doing what he was created to do. Just as a bird flies, for that is his nature, and an ox pulls wagons and machinery with his strength, similarly, a wise man is using his natural abilities. Someone who isn't as smart as he would be smarter had he possessed his level of intellect" (*Mesillat Yesharim* 22).

178. Arrogance assumes many forms; it is insidious, and it can seep in and out everywhere. We must be aware that our ego, regardless of our good intentions, betrays us. For instance, let's imagine that we are feeling upset with someone, but we tell ourselves, "I won't get angry at this person." Such thinking is a corruption of reality, and we impede our ability to remain calm. Why? When we rely solely on ourselves, without any input from God, no matter how noble the pursuit, we foster arrogance, and we are divided by our ego even before we begin. While it is true that we can be successful with this form of thinking, it is more taxing and less precise than the thought, "I do not wish to get angry, it is my will to remain calm. . . . God, please let it be Your will that allows me to exercise self-control." When we use our will to ask God to help us, and fulfill our wishes, we remain whole and tapped into the Infinite.

179. Of course, there are arrogant people who are successful, according to society's definition of success. The age-old question of why it is that

When we fail to utilize our potential, and pursue instead frivolous distractions, we are displaying a profound lack of gratitude.[180] Everything in creation has a positive reason for being,[181] or it would not exist.[182]

---

good people go through such hardships while the bad seem to prosper is beyond the scope of this work. Indeed, perhaps it is beyond the scope of our understanding; as Rabbi Yannai said, "It is not in our power to explain the tranquility of the wicked or the suffering of the righteous" (Ethics of the Fathers 4:19). That said, God's judgment is absolute and just, whether or not it meets with our understanding. The surface explanation, however, is that the reason God allows a person to have success is that sometimes God will reward a person here, in this world, for any good he may have done, so that he will not merit to receive reward in the world to come. This person, however, does suffer emotionally, and, despite appearances, he is not and cannot be truly happy if he is so arrogant.

180. Moses tells the Jewish people that after they enter the Land of Israel they must: "Take care lest your forget the Lord, your God . . . and you build good houses and . . . you increase silver and gold . . . and everything you have will increase . . . and you will forget the Lord, your God, who took you out of . . . Egypt from a house of slavery . . ." (Deuteronomy 8:11–14). Moses pleads with the Jewish people that when *"everything you have will increase,"* don't forget the One who gave it to you.

181. "Everything He created, is good for its time" (Ecclesiastes 3).

182. The Yalkut (Samuel 131) tells how King David complained to God, asking why there were crazy people in the world who tear their hair out and create a nuisance. God swore to him that he, too, would act in such a way during his lifetime. When King David ran away from King Saul to Gat, Achish, the king of Gat, wanted to kill him. King David started acting crazy until Achish threw him out of the palace. King David then said, "I will bless God at all times" (Psalms 34:2).

If we misuse, abuse, or ignore a gift then our soul disconnects from God (as a fail-safe, a person becomes unhappy, anxious, and insecure) in order to wake us up to our actions.[183]

183. Since everything in our world has the potential to bring us closer to God, the same gift may take on a new purpose, or may exist for the same purpose while taking a more circuitous, possibly painful, route.

CHAPTER 15

LETTING GOD CREATE OUR DAY

"On the path one is determined to go, God leads him."

—MAKKOT 10B

The essence of matter lies in its shape as well as its function. The letters of the Hebrew alphabet illustrates this truth beautifully where the shape of each letter reveals its identity.[184] It is the synergy of form and function that maximizes its energy. Think about it. If the design of something is in accord with its purpose, then it does not

---

184. Correspondingly, in *Lashon Hakodesh*, the word describes the very essence of the person or object. At the time of creation, all the animals were brought before Adam in order to be named. "And whatever Adam called it, that was its name" (Genesis 2:19). We find that the animal did not simply receive a name in this "ceremony" of sorts; rather that *was* its name. Adam perceived the very essence of each animal, and was therefore able to *know* its name.

have to do anything to utilize or even maximize its potential. It simply exists.

To arrive at form following function, the vessel that contains us must also be that which fills us. Consequently, there is no waste, and no energy is lost.[185] When doing what is right comes naturally, we change less and reach a theoretical conclusion where we do good merely because that is who we are—like God.[186]

BEING REAL

We simply cannot pretend or try to be something else and have it be so. An echo depends on the physical dimensions of an object to reflect sound. A picture of a cave does not produce an echo. The cave needs to be real. A person may be hypnotized into believing that he

134

185. A sphere—a bubble, a planet, the sun—is the most basic shape in nature, yet this is the shape that maximizes space—the volume-to-surface area ratio. According to The Ari, when God constricted His infinite light in the process of creation, the vacated space was perfectly spherical (*Etz Chaim* 1:1:2, p. 27f). The spherical description is a kabbalistic representation and is not to be interpreted as a physical depiction.

186. *Michtav Me'Eliyahu* expounds on this (vol. 1, p. 115), stating that one does receive a reward every time he performs a *mitzvah*, even if it is seemingly part of his character. He doesn't need to convince himself to do the right thing, for he has previously developed this level of consciousness, and made it a part of his being.

is a cow and he will moo on command. Giving milk, however, is an entirely separate issue.

The more we resemble our Creator, by emulating His ways, the greater is our connection with God. This is because closeness is not measured in terms of physical space, but through levels of awareness that manifest from similarities.[187] We should not see our relationship with God as two halves coming together. Only that which is whole can integrate into the Whole.[188]

When we say that God is One, indeed everything is one because He created it all. The energy that preceded matter is made up of the same universal "stuff." It is only when form is given that the illusion of separateness emerges. When we lose our false selves, we gain a fluid identity. We become, in a word, formless, and at this level, we are as close to God as we possibly can be.[189] This brings us to the definitive payoff.

While clear and direct communication with God is not possible, because we exist on a lower spiritual level

---

187. *Derech HaShem* (1:1:2).
188. Maimonides (*Hilchot Yesodei Hatorah* 1:6).
189. If we could theoretically match God's frequency, then we would literally be moved by Him. In the physical world, all matter resonates at the natural vibrating frequency of each respective object. If a singer emits a note at a minimum of 135 decibels for at least a few seconds, the vibration can build up enough energy to shatter a glass. Whereas the human voice has limitations, a machine can accomplish this feat easily and reliably.

than our forefathers, there exists, even today, a form of Divine intuition—where the soul and God intersect.[190]

It often manifests in a hunch, sixth sense, or gut instinct. Without intense thought, we just "know" what to do, or perhaps even know what is going to happen. At that moment, we gain access to Infinite intelligence, and the correct path is illuminated, in magnified detail.

We can extend this moment into every moment, by exercising the only power that a human being possesses: free will. As we continue to rise above our nature, the better we can see, hear, and understand the subtleties, intricacies, and facets of God's plan for us and the world. God is *constantly* speaking to us, but it is our responsibility to keep the lines of communication open.[191]

---

190. God and man's higher soul both share the same purpose, the same desire, and the same will. So the often-asked question, "Does God swoop in and interfere with our free will?" becomes meaningless. The real us (our souls) and God are together. They battle the forces that are only illusions of who we are: our bodies and our egos. These forces exist solely to challenge us in order to help us to reach our potential. It is like asking, "Who is in charge, your right hand or your left hand?" Of course, they are both under the domain of your brain, working towards a common objective.

191. If someone prays for mercy on behalf of another when he himself needs that very same thing, he is answered first (*Bava Kamma* 92a). We understand this statement beautifully in the context of a situation in which the person's ego is not engaged and so he is therefore closer to God. Because communication with God operates in both directions at the same time, our ability to both hear and speak pivots on our capacity to do so with minimum interference.

CONCLUSION

The Talmud recounts the story of Elazar Ben Dordaya, who wished to repent after years of self-indulgence and decadence.[192] First Elazar cried out to the mountains and hills:

"Mountains and hills, ask mercy for me."

We can gain insight into Elazar's plea by examining the Hebrew word for mountain, *harim*, which can be interpreted as *horim*, parents. In other words, instead of taking responsibility for his behavior, Elazar Ben Dordaya blamed his parents, who brought him into this world.

If we take a look at ourselves and the people in our lives, many of us are guilty of a similar attitude. We blame our upbringing, our parents, our education . . .

---

192. *Avoda Zara* 17a.

anything or anyone, *but ourselves.* Accordingly, Elazar's entreaties were denied:

"Ask mercy for you? We must ask mercy for ourselves."

Next, Elazar turned to heaven and earth, which symbolized the times in which he lived, and the people with whom he associated:

"Heaven and earth, ask mercy for me."

"I could not have been anything else; I am a product of my environment. Why am I to blame?" In vain, Elazar sought to blame the heavens and the earth, and his request was rejected:

"Ask mercy for you? We must ask for ourselves."

Elazar further declared, "Sun and moon, ask mercy for me."

According to commentators, the sun and moon symbolize the riches and affluence of society. Elazar exclaimed: "I was enticed and became ensnared in this lifestyle." Once again, his plea was dismissed:

"Ask mercy for you? We must ask mercy for ourselves."

Finally, at the height of despair, Eleazar cried out to the stars and planets, symbols of a predestined fate.

"Stars and planets, ask mercy for me. I did not have *mazal.* I am a victim of fate and circumstance."[193] Of

---

193. "A Jew is not bound by mazal, but ascends above it" (*Shabbat* 156a).

course, his final plea was rejected by the stars and the planets:

"Ask mercy for you? We must ask mercy for ourselves."

Feeling utterly helpless, Elazar went and sat down between two mountains and two valleys, and, after a long and serious period of probing introspection, he placed his head between his knees and realized that there is no one but himself to blame for his actions. Finally, in anguish, he cried out, "It all depends on me—the responsibility is totally mine!"[194]

IN THE END

We are responsible for our satisfaction with life, whether we choose to accept this or not. If we accept responsibility for our lives, then nothing can stop us; if we do not, then nothing will move us.

194. At that moment, the Talmud concludes that a heavenly voice proclaimed: "Elazar ben Dordaya is worthy of Eternal Life."

ACKNOWLEDGEMENTS

This work was made possible because of the cooperation, support, and expertise, of many people.

I am grateful to Hagoan Harav Shmuel Kamenetsky Sh'lita, who showed confidence in this project.

To the legendary, incomparable Rabbi Ronnie Greenwald for his continuous interest and help with this book, I owe my admiration and gratitude.

It is with deep appreciation that I acknowledge Rabbi Moshe Goldberger for his tremendous input, insights, and observations. This book has been improved because of his many contributions.

Thank you to Hagoan Harav Dovid Cohen Sh'lita, whose warmth and graciousness is matched only by his wisdom. Thank you to Rabbi Abraham J. Twerski, MD, Rabbi Yaakov Salomon, Rabbi Zelig Pliskin, Rabbi Leib

Kelemen, Rabbi Paysach Krohn, and Dr. Michael J. Salamon. I am grateful for their time, kind words, and interest in this project.

Many thanks to Rabbi Moshe Rockove for offering added sources and commentary, and to David Grossman for his editorial assistance. A resounding thank you to my extraordinary editor, Sorelle Weinstein, who helped transform this book into a concise and cogent work.

I am forever indebted to Rabbi Noah Weinberg, founder and dean of Aish HaTorah, for all that he has done for my family and myself.

To Eva Levi, an army of one who does so much good for so many, I offer endless thanks and continued appreciation. Thanks, too, to Rabbi Aryeh Leib Nivin, Rabbi Mark Spiro, Rabbi Yitz Greenman, Rabbi Ezriel Munk, and Rabbi Moshe Katz for their ongoing availability and counsel.

Thank you to my parents whose encouragement, inspiration, and love continue to infuse me with the ability to become more than what I am. As well, thank you to my terrific in-laws for their never-ceasing thoughtfulness, and to my brothers for their precision insight, and advice.

Finally, I owe everything I am, and ever will be and do, to HaKadosh Baruch Hu, Whose infinite kindness and generosity have allowed this book to unfold, and Who has blessed me with my wife, Shira, and my children, who make it all possible and worthwhile.

Please Note

While this book has been vetted to offer information that is sound in *hashkafa*, if you find anything objectionable, please bear in mind that this in no way reflects upon the integrity of those individuals who offered their kind words to this book and who lent their names in support. Editorial changes may have affected content that no longer supports their position or opinion. *Sole responsibility for any errors, omissions, or inconsistencies lie with the author.* To this end, any comments, suggestions, and corrections are welcome so that this work can be revised for future editions.

BIOGRAPHICAL DETAILS OF FAMOUS JEWISH THINKERS AND RABBIS NOTED IN THIS WORK

Rabbi Akiva (Akiva ben Joseph). c.50–135 C.E. One of the principal figures in the Mishnah and Talmud.

Rashi. 1040–1105. Rabbi Shlomo Yitzhaki. Greatest Jewish biblical commentator, from Troyes, France.

Rambam (Maimonides, Rabbi Moshe ben Maimon). 1135–1204. One of the greatest Jewish thinkers of all time. Active mostly in Spain and Egypt.

Ramban (Nachmanides, Rabbi Moshe ben Nachman). 1194–1270. Great biblical commentator and Jewish communal leader in Spain.

Rabbi Ovadiah Sforno. 1475–1550. Italian Bible commentator and physician.

The Maharal (Rabbi Judah Loew). 1525–1609. One of the most seminal Jewish thinkers in the post-medieval period.

The Ari (Rabbi Yitzchak Luria). 1534–1572. A great Kabbalist in Safed.

Rabbi Moshe Chaim Luzzatto. 1707–1746. A prominent Italian Jewish rabbi and philosopher, best remembered for his ethical treatise *Mesillat Yesharim* (Path of the Just).

Vilna Gaon. 1720–1797. Rabbi Elijah of Vilna. The *gaon* ("genius") of Vilna, one of the greatest Talmudic thinkers of all time.

Levi Yitzchok of Berdichev. 1740–1810. Early Hasidic Master, who taught in Britchval, Zelichav, and Pinsk, as well as Berdichev.

Rabbi Yaakov Tzvi Mecklenburg. 1785–1865. Bible commentator. Poland

Rav Leib Chasman. He was hired in 1897 as the *mussar mashgiach* (ethical teacher) at the famous Telshe yeshiva, and later achieved world renown as the senior *mussar mashgiach* at the Hebron Yeshiva in Jerusalem.

Chofetz Chaim (Rabbi Israel Meir Hacohen Kagan). 1838–1933. An influential Eastern European rabbi, Halachist, and ethicist, whose works continue to be widely influential in Jewish life.

The Alter of Slabodka (Rabbi Nosson Tzvi Finkel). 1849–1927. An influential leader of Orthodox Judaism in Eastern Europe, founder of the Slabodka Yeshiva in the town of Slabodka.

Rabbi Shneur Kotler. 1918–1982. Son of the famed Talmudic scholar Rabbi Aharon Kotler. Upon the death of his father in 1962, he became the Rosh Yeshiva of Beis Medrash Govoha in Lakewood, New Jersey.

Rabbi Avraham Yaakov Pam. 1913–2001. Began his career at Yeshiva Torah Vodaas in 1938, and held many positions, including Rosh Yeshiva, over more than sixty years.

GLOSSARY

Adam Harishon – the first man

Anav – Humble person

Avraham Avinu – The biblical patriarch, Abraham

Ayin tova – Being satisfied with what you have

Ba'al bitachon – Someone who recognizes God's role in the workings of this world

Beit Din – Rabbinical court

Berachot – Tract of the Talmud dealing with blessings

Bitachon – Trust

Cheshbon Hanefesh – Spiritual accounting

Cholei Haguf – People who suffer from physical afflictions

Cholei Hanefesh – People who suffer from emotional or spiritual sickness

Chovot Halevavot – A famous ethical work by Rabbi

Bachya Ibn Pakudah (eleventh century, Spain),
presenting the ethical teachings of Judaism

Da'at – One of the ten *sefirot* (see *sefirah*), *da'at* is the
sefirah of knowledge

Emunah – Faith

Even Shleimah – A compendium of wisdom by the Gaon
of Vilna (see appendix)

Gemara – The second part of the Talmud consisting
primarily of commentary on the Mishnah, as well as
vast anecdotal material teaching moral and practical
lessons of life.

Gezeira Milmaala – A heavenly decree

Gilgul –Reincarnation

Haktav Vehakabbalah – Torah commentary authored by
Rabbi Tzvi Mecklenburg

Halachah – Jewish law

Havdalah – Literally, separation

Kabbalah – Literally, receiving or tradition, Kabbalah is
the esoteric dimension of the Torah

Lashon Hakodesh – Holy tongue, Hebrew language

Masecha (pl. *Masechtot*) – Volume

Megillat Esther – The Book of Esther that contains the
story of Purim

Mesillat Yesharim – An ethical text composed in 1740 by
the influential Rabbi Moshe Chaim Luzzatto
(1707–1746)

Michtav M'eliyahu – Rabbi Eliyahu Dessler's classic ethical work

Middah (pl. *Middot*) – Character trait

Midrash – Early rabbinic compendium of legal or narrative material

Mitzvah (pl. *Mitzvot*) – Commandment

Mishnah – Main source of the Oral Torah, later compiled into six volumes by Yehuda Hanassi

Nefesh – Soul

Nefesh Shfela – Personality to get along well with people

Neshama – Soul

Orchot Tzaddikim – A book on Jewish ethics written in Germany in the fifteenth century

Parnossa – Livelihood

Rasha – Evil person

Ruach Nemucha – Humility

Sanhedrin – Jewish supreme court

Sefirah (pl. *sefirot*) – A *sefirah* is a channel of Divine energy or life-force. It is through the *sefirot* that God interacts with creation. They may therefore be considered His "attributes."

Sha'ar Habitachon – A chapter in *Chovot HaLevavot*, Duties of the Heart, by Rabbi Bachya Ibn Pakudah

Shemittah – Jewish sabbatical year

Shemoneh Perakim – Rambam's introduction to his commentary on Ethics of the Fathers

Shulchan Aruch – The Code of Jewish Law, authored by Rabbi Joseph Karo in the fifteenth century

Talmud – Largest compilation of Jewish writings of numerous volumes, in which all of Jewish law and thought is represented in mainly dialogue form

Tanach – Complete Jewish Bible

Teshuvah – Repentance

Tzaddik – Righteous person

Tzimtzum – Contraction and "removal" of God's infinite light in order to allow for creation of independent realities

Tzora'at – Physical affliction akin to leprosy

Yetzer Hora – Evil inclination

Yalkut – Aggadic compilation on the books of the Old Testament

Yetzer tov – Good inclination; moral conscience that reminds a person of God's laws when faced with a choice of how to behave

Vitry Machzor – Contains decisions and rulings, as well as *responsa* by Rashi and other authorities

Zerizut – Energetic action

ABOUT THE AUTHOR

DOVID LIEBERMAN, PH.D., is an award-winning author and internationally recognized leader in the field of human behavior and interpersonal relationships. Techniques based on his seven books, which have been translated into eighteen languages and include two New York Times best-sellers, are used by the FBI, The Department of the Navy, FORTUNE 500 companies, and by governments, corporations and mental health professionals in more than twenty-five countries. He has appeared as a guest expert on more than 200 programs such as, The Today Show, Fox News, and The View, and his works have been featured in publications around the world.

Blending Torah wisdom with the psychological process, Dovid Lieberman's talks are enjoyed by people at all levels, and from all backgrounds—frum and kiruvoriented alike—and include: parenting, shalom bayit (household harmony), relationships, Judaism, self-esteem, singles topics, spirituality, success, psychology, teens, family, education, and counseling. He writes a bi-weekly column called "Human Nature 101" for The Jewish Press. He lives in Lakewood, New Jersey, with his wife and children.

You can contact the author by email: DavidJay@aol.com or visit www.David613.com for updates and additional information.

·KEYNOTE ADDRESSES·
·LECTURES & WORKSHOPS·

Spanning a spectrum of venues, from Agudah to Chabad and AJOP to Kollel's worldwide, Dr. Lieberman is a highly sought-after speaker, whose engaging and interactive style is enjoyed by people at all levels and backgrounds.

TOPICS INCLUDE:
- Parenting • Shalom Bayis • Relationships • Judiasm
- Self-Esteem • Singles Topics • Education • Conflict Resolution
- Anger & Stress Management • Teens
- Human Nature • Counseling • Kiruv

**Invite Dr. Lieberman to your
community or organization.**

"Dr. Lieberman's blend of Jewish and psychological insights, together with his presentation skills, make him one of the most dynamic speakers that I've ever seen or heard."

—Rabbi Yehoshua Kohl
Director of Education and Programming, Gateways

"Dr. Lieberman is our leadoff speaker every semester at our Maimonides program at Rutgers . . . the students love him!"

—Rabbi Meir Goldberg, Director, RJX

"Dr. Lieberman brings an audience to life! He's spoken at our branches and by Shabbatons more than two dozen times."

—Rabbi Yitz Greenman
Executive Director, Aish HaTorah Discovery

"Dr. Lieberman has 'street credibility' and his bio alone brings people in the doors. He's highly relatable and entertaining, but delivers a potent message the way few can . . . he's probably the best all-around speaker I've ever heard, on any subject."

—Rabbi Moshe Katz
Director of Personnel and Training, Torah Links

Email DJLMedia@aol.com   Fax 772-619-7828

·TELE-SEMINARS·

Registration is now open for an exciting new workshop series covering a range of relationship and personal development topics, including: shalom bayis, practical parenting, conflict resolution, and self-esteem.

The program offers a range of techniques and tools distilled from Torah wisdom and psychological principles that professionals and laymen alike can use to increase emotional wellbeing and improve relationships. Participants will come away with a deeper understanding of human-nature and interpersonal relationships.

All lectures are interactive, live, and over the phone—so you can participate from the comfort and convenience of your home or anywhere; plus, you can ask questions in real-time or email or call ahead of time.

Join our progress-oriented program, with practical solutions to real problems.